" EYES IN THE SHADOW YOUR BLUEPRINT FOR CORPORATE DOMINANCE"

CHENNAMALLIKARJUN C BHUSANUR

Made with ♥ on the Notion Press Platform
www.notionpress.com

In loving memory of my father, the late Shri Channabasappa
Bhusanur, whose meticulous record-keeping instilled in me a deep
appreciation for detail. And to my mother, the late Smt. Umadevi,
whose gift of clear expression ignited my passion for articulation.
From you both, I inherit the qualities that have shaped my journey —
keen observation and the ability to translate it into meaningful words.

Contents

Preface   *ix*

Acknowledgements   *xi*

Section 1: Foundations Of Management And Organization

1. The Human Body As A Blueprint For Organizational Success   3
2. Types Of Management Theories   11
3. Intellect And Intelligence In Management Functions   18
4. The Dual Role Of Leadership: Prevention And Correction   23
5. Organizational Setbacks: Internal And External Challenges   26

Section 2: Tools And Techniques For Effective Management

6. The Role Of Relevant Information In Efficient Contingency Management   31
7. The Power Of Lateral Thinking In Leadership And Investigations   35
8. Integrating Lateral Thinking Into Organizations   38
9. Talent Poaching: A Silent Corporate Threat   41
10. Crisis Management: Investigating The Storm   44

Section 3: Investigative Techniques And Corporate Security

Contents

11. The Role Of Private Investigators In Management — 51

12. The Role Of Private Investigators In Various Contingencies — 54

13. Corporate Investigations: A Deeper Dive With Indian Case Studies — 58

14. Undercover Operations: A Double-Edged Sword — 62

15. Undercover Operations In The Healthcare Industry — 65

16. Undercover Operations In Corporate Investigations — 70

17. The Undercover Operation And Entrapment — 74

18. Surveillance: A Double-Edged Sword — 79

19. Challenges In Implementing Surveillance Programs — 84

20. Surveillance In The IT Industry — 87

21. Surveillance In The Manufacturing Industry — 90

22. Surveillance Technologies In Manufacturing — 94

23. Video Analytics: The Intelligence Behind The Camera — 98

24. Challenges In Implementing Surveillance Systems — 101

25. Overcoming The Challenge Of False Positives In Surveillance Systems — 105

Contents

26. False Positives In The Financial Industry   107

27. False Positives In The Insurance Industry   109

28. False Positives In Cybersecurity   111

Section 4: Screening And Due Diligence

29. Application Of Screening In Business Practice   115

30. Screening As A Corporate Safeguard   118

31. In-House Screening Vs. Professional Investigators   121

32. Screening In The Entertainment Industry   124

33. Customer Due Diligence (CDD) In The Financial Services Industry   126

34. Screening In Litigation Support Services   129

35. The Advantages Of Employing A Private Investigator For Corporate Investigations   133

Legal And Regulatory Framework

36. Changes Brought By The Bhartiya Sakshya Sanhita   139

Glossary: -   143

Relevant Resources for the Book   145

Preface

The labyrinthine corridors of the corporate world are often shrouded in shadows, where subtle strategies and keen insights hold the key to success. *Eyes in the Shadow: Your Blueprint for Corporate Dominance* is an invitation to illuminate those shadowy corners. It is a culmination of years of observation, research, and practical experience in the realm of corporate investigations and security.

I am indebted to my colleagues, friends, and the numerous professionals who have contributed to the shaping of this work through insightful discussions and invaluable suggestions. Their expertise has been instrumental in illuminating the complexities of the corporate landscape. To my family, whose unwavering support and patience have been my constant companions throughout this endeavor, I extend my deepest gratitude.

This book would not have been possible without the aid of advanced AI platforms, which accelerated the research and writing process. Their capacity to process vast amounts of information and identify patterns was invaluable.

This book is more than just a manual; it is a compass, guiding you through the intricate maze of corporate strategy. It is a tool to empower you to see beyond the obvious, to anticipate challenges, and to seize opportunities. Let us embark on this journey together, into the shadows that hold the secrets to corporate dominance.

Acknowledgements

This book "Eyes in the Shadow your blueprint for Corporate dominance" is a culmination of years of experience, research, and insights gleaned from the intricate world of investigations and corporate strategy. As I embark on this literary journey, I am deeply indebted to the unwavering support of my family and friends whose encouragement has been the bedrock of this endeavor. Their patience and belief in my abilities have been an invaluable source of strength.

I extend my sincere gratitude to the readers of my previous work, Undercover Chronicles, whose enthusiasm and feedback inspired me to delve deeper into the complexities of the corporate world. Your belief in my ability to offer valuable insights has been a constant motivation.

The advancement of technology, particularly the role of AI in information processing and analysis, has been instrumental in shaping this book. I acknowledge the contribution of these technological advancements in making this work a reality.

Lastly, I would like to thank the countless professionals, colleagues, and clients who have shared their experiences and knowledge with me over the years. Your insights have enriched my understanding of the corporate landscape and have been invaluable in crafting this book.

Section 1: Foundations of Management and Organization

1. The Human Body as a Blueprint for Organizational Success
2. Types of Management Theories A Contingent Approach in the Age of AI and Human Influence
3. Intellect and Intelligence in Management Functions
4. The Dual Role of Leadership: Prevention and Correction
5. Organizational Setbacks: Internal and External Challenges

CHAPTER ONE

The Human Body as a Blueprint for Organizational Success

The Human Body as an Organization

- **The Brain as Leadership:** The brain, the command center, is akin to organizational leadership. It processes information, makes decisions, and coordinates various functions.
- **The Skeleton as Structure:** The skeletal system provides structure and support, much like an organization's hierarchy and departments.
- **The Circulatory System as Supply Chain:** The heart pumps blood (resources) throughout the body (organization), ensuring all parts function optimally.
- **The Immune System as Risk Management:** The immune system protects the body from external threats, similar to an organization's risk management function.
- **Digestive System as Operations:** Breaking down complex inputs (raw materials) into usable energy (products or services) mirrors an organization's

operations.

- **Muscles as Workforce:** The muscles carry out the work, analogous to an organization's employees.
- **Skin as Public Image:** The body's outer layer represents an organization's public image, protecting the internal functions and reflecting its health.

Implications for Management

Understanding these parallels can inform management strategies:

- **Holistic Perspective:** Just as the body is interconnected, organizations must consider all components for optimal performance.
- **Employee Well-being:** Similar to physical health, employee well-being is crucial for organizational success.
- **Adaptability:** Like the body adapting to changes, organizations must be agile to thrive.
- **Continuous Improvement:** Just as the body repairs and regenerates, organizations must continuously evolve.

By viewing an organization through the lens of the human body, leaders can gain fresh perspectives on challenges and opportunities.

The Human Body and the Corporation: A Comparative Analysis of Health and Performance

The human body, a complex system of interconnected organs and tissues, requires meticulous care to function optimally. Similarly, a corporation, a complex system of interconnected departments and functions, necessitates strategic management to achieve its goals. Both entities face a spectrum of threats, both internal and external, and require a combination of preventive and corrective measures to maintain their health and performance.

Internal Threats

Just as the human body is susceptible to internal disorders like heart disease, diabetes, or cancer, a corporation can be plagued by internal issues such as poor leadership, toxic culture, or financial mismanagement.

- **Leadership:** A weak or ineffective leader, much like a malfunctioning brain, can paralyze an organization. This can manifest in poor decision-making, lack of vision, or inability to inspire employees.
- **Organizational Culture:** A toxic culture, characterized by fear, mistrust, or lack of collaboration, can hinder innovation, productivity, and employee morale. It is akin to a body with a compromised immune system, vulnerable to infections.
- **Financial Health:** Poor financial management, such as excessive debt, inefficient spending, or lack of cash flow, can lead to financial instability and even bankruptcy. This is comparable to a body with malnutrition.

External Threats

Both the human body and a corporation face external challenges. For the human body, these include environmental pollutants, infectious diseases, and accidents. For a corporation, these encompass economic downturns, competitor actions, regulatory changes, and technological disruptions.

- **Economic Conditions:** A recession or economic downturn can impact a corporation's revenue, profitability, and market share. This is similar to a body's weakened resistance to infections during periods of malnutrition.
- **Competition:** Intense competition can erode market share and profitability. Just as a body is vulnerable to attacks from external pathogens, a corporation can be susceptible to competitive pressures.
- **Regulatory Environment:** Changes in government regulations can impact a corporation's operations, costs, and revenue. This is comparable to environmental factors affecting human health.

Preventive Measures

Both the human body and a corporation benefit from preventive measures. For the human body, this includes a balanced diet, regular exercise, and preventive healthcare. For a corporation, strategic planning, talent development, and risk management are essential.

- **Strategic Planning:** A well-defined corporate strategy is akin to a roadmap for the body's health. It guides decision-making, resource allocation, and overall direction.
- **Talent Development:** Investing in employee development ensures a skilled and motivated workforce. This is comparable to maintaining physical fitness through regular exercise.
- **Risk Management:** Identifying and mitigating potential risks is crucial for both individuals and corporations. It is similar to preventive healthcare measures like vaccinations.

Corrective Actions

When faced with challenges, both the human body and a corporation require timely and effective corrective actions. For the human body, this includes medication, surgery, or lifestyle changes. For a corporation, restructuring, mergers, or acquisitions might be necessary.

- **Restructuring:** Eliminating inefficiencies, streamlining operations, and downsizing can help a corporation regain its financial health. This is similar to surgical procedures to remove diseased tissue.
- **Mergers and Acquisitions:** Combining forces with another company can provide access to new markets, technologies, or talent. This is comparable to organ transplantation.
- **Change Management:** Implementing significant changes within an organization can be challenging. Effective change management is crucial for a smooth transition.

In conclusion, the human body and a corporation share remarkable similarities in terms of their structures, functions, challenges, and management strategies. By understanding these parallels, leaders can adopt a holistic approach to organizational health, focusing on both prevention and correction. Just as a healthcare professional cares for the overall well-being of a patient, effective leaders must nurture the health and vitality of their organizations.

By proactively addressing internal and external threats, investing in preventive measures, and implementing corrective actions when necessary, corporations can enhance their resilience, adaptability, and long-term success.

The Human Body, the Organization, and Their Respective Threats

Building upon the analogy of the human body and an organization, it's evident that both entities are susceptible to their own unique set of threats. Just as the human body is vulnerable to diseases, an organization faces a myriad of challenges that can impede its growth and success.

A human body is a complex ecosystem, constantly under siege from pathogens like bacteria, viruses, and parasites. These invaders disrupt the body's homeostasis, leading to illness or even death. Similarly, organizations operate in a competitive and dynamic environment, facing threats such as economic downturns, technological disruptions, and shifts in consumer preferences. These challenges can destabilize an organization, leading to financial losses, market share decline, or even bankruptcy.

Much like the immune system protects the body from external threats, an organization's risk management function serves as its defense mechanism. A robust immune system identifies and neutralizes pathogens, preventing them from causing harm. Likewise, a well-structured risk management framework helps an organization identify potential threats, assess their impact, and develop mitigation strategies.

For instance, a virus attacking the respiratory system can be compared to a cyberattack targeting an organization's IT infrastructure. Both threats can cause significant damage, disrupt operations, and compromise sensitive information. In both cases, prevention, detection, and swift response are crucial.

Furthermore, chronic diseases like diabetes or heart disease can gradually weaken the body's functions, impacting overall health. Similarly, organizational diseases such as bureaucracy, complacency, or toxic culture can erode efficiency, innovation, and employee morale. These chronic issues can be difficult to address but require persistent attention and remedial actions.

The analogy also extends to the concept of preventative care. Regular check-ups, vaccinations, and healthy lifestyle choices help maintain bodily health. In the organizational context, strategic planning, employee development, and market research are akin to preventative measures. By proactively identifying potential issues and taking steps to address them, organizations can enhance their resilience and adaptability.

Just as a balanced diet and regular exercise contribute to overall well-being, a healthy organizational culture, strong leadership, and effective talent management are essential for long-term success. These factors boost employee morale, foster innovation, and enhance the organization's ability to weather storms.

In conclusion, the human body and an organization are both complex systems vulnerable to various threats. By understanding the parallels between these two entities, leaders can develop effective strategies to protect and strengthen their organizations. Just as healthcare professionals work tirelessly to safeguard human health, leaders must be vigilant in identifying and mitigating risks to ensure the long-term success and sustainability of their businesses.

By adopting a holistic approach that focuses on prevention, early detection, and rapid response, organizations can build resilience and emerge stronger from even the most challenging circumstances.

CHAPTER TWO

Types of Management Theories

Management theories have evolved over time, reflecting the changing nature of organizations and work. They provide frameworks for understanding and addressing managerial challenges.

Classical Management Theory

This theory emerged during the Industrial Revolution and focuses on efficiency and productivity. It comprises two primary branches:

- **Scientific Management:** Pioneered by Frederick Winslow Taylor, this theory emphasizes the application of scientific methods to improve efficiency in production processes. It involves task analysis, time and motion studies, and worker selection and training to optimize performance.

- **Administrative Management:** Developed by Henri Fayol, this theory concentrates on the overall management of an organization rather than individual tasks. It outlines principles such as division of labor, authority, discipline, unity of command, and unity of direction.

Bureaucratic Management Theory

Max Weber contributed significantly to this theory, emphasizing the importance of formal rules, procedures, and hierarchies. Bureaucracy aims to create efficient and predictable organizations through clear roles, responsibilities, and decision-making processes. While it can lead to efficiency, it can also stifle creativity and flexibility.

Human Relations Theory

A reaction to the mechanistic approach of classical theories, this theory focuses on the human element in organizations. It emphasizes the importance of employee morale, motivation, and social interactions. Elton Mayo's Hawthorne studies highlighted the impact of social factors on productivity. This theory paved the way for more humanistic approaches to management.

Systems Management Theory

This theory views organizations as open systems interacting with their environment. It emphasizes the interconnectedness of different parts of an organization and the importance of synergy. Systems theory encourages managers to consider the broader context of their decisions and to focus on achieving organizational goals through coordinated efforts.

Contingency Management Theory

Recognizing that there is no one-size-fits-all approach to management, contingency theory suggests that the best management style depends on the specific situation. Factors such as organizational size, industry, technology, and environmental conditions influence the most effective management approach.

Theory X and Theory Y

Douglas McGregor proposed these two contrasting theories about human nature and its implications for management.

- **Theory X:** Assumes that employees are inherently lazy, dislike work, and need to be coerced, controlled, and threatened with punishment to achieve organizational goals.
- **Theory Y:** Assumes that employees are motivated, creative, and seek responsibility. This theory emphasizes participative management, job enrichment, and employee empowerment.

Conclusion

Management theories offer valuable insights into organizational behavior and performance. While each theory has its strengths and limitations, they collectively contribute to our understanding of effective management practices. Modern management often incorporates elements from various theories to address the complexities of contemporary organizations. It is essential to recognize that the best approach depends on the specific context and the organization's goals.

By understanding these theories, managers can develop a broader perspective, make informed decisions, and adapt their leadership styles to meet the challenges of a changing business environment.

A Contingent Approach in the Age of AI and Human Influence

The evolution of management thought, from the rigid structures of Classical Management Theory to the people-centric focus of Human Relations Theory, has been a journey of adaptation and refinement. However, the contemporary business landscape, characterized by rapid technological advancements and a dynamic global economy, demands a more nuanced approach. Contingency Management Theory, with its emphasis on flexibility and situational awareness, emerges as a foundational framework for modern leadership.

The Limitations of Classical and Human Relations Theories

Classical Management Theory, while instrumental in establishing foundational management principles, often overlooks the human element and the complexities of modern organizations. Its rigid structures and emphasis on efficiency can stifle innovation and adaptability. On the other hand, Human Relations Theory, while recognizing the importance of employee morale and motivation, may fall short in providing a comprehensive framework for managing complex organizational challenges.

The Rise of Contingency Management Theory

Contingency Management Theory offers a more pragmatic perspective. It acknowledges that there is no universal "best way" to manage and that effective leadership depends on various factors, including organizational size, culture, technology, and external environment. This theory encourages leaders to analyze specific situations and adopt management styles and strategies accordingly.

For instance, a startup operating in a highly competitive, fast-paced industry might benefit from a more decentralized and entrepreneurial approach, emphasizing employee empowerment and innovation. In contrast, a large, established corporation operating in a regulated industry might require a more centralized and bureaucratic structure to ensure efficiency and compliance.

The Influence of AI and Human Factors

The convergence of artificial intelligence (AI) and human influence is reshaping the workplace. AI-driven automation is transforming tasks, roles, and organizational structures. Simultaneously, the growing emphasis on employee well-being, diversity, and inclusion is influencing management practices.

AI Influence:

- **Data-Driven Decision Making:** AI enables leaders to analyze vast amounts of data to make informed decisions. For example, a retail company can use AI to predict customer behavior, optimize inventory management, and personalize marketing campaigns.
- **Automation and Process Optimization:** AI can automate routine tasks, freeing up employees to focus on higher-value activities. For instance, AI-powered chatbots can handle customer inquiries, improving efficiency and customer satisfaction.
- **New Business Models:** AI is driving the creation of new business models. For example, AI-driven platforms are disrupting industries such as transportation, finance, and healthcare.

Human Influence:

- **Employee Experience:** As technology advances, the importance of human connection and employee well-being increases. Leaders must focus on creating a positive work environment, fostering employee engagement, and developing talent.

- **Diversity and Inclusion:** Building diverse and inclusive teams is essential for innovation and problem-solving. Leaders must create a culture where everyone feels valued and empowered to contribute.
- **Ethical Considerations:** The use of AI raises ethical concerns. Leaders must ensure that AI is used responsibly and ethically, considering the impact on employees, customers, and society.

A Hybrid Approach

To navigate this complex landscape, leaders must adopt a hybrid approach that combines elements of different management theories. While contingency management provides a foundational framework, incorporating insights from classical and human relations theories is essential.

For example, a leader might use elements of scientific management to optimize operational efficiency while also focusing on employee well-being as advocated by human relations theory. At the same time, a contingency approach would be applied to determine the optimal balance between these two perspectives based on the specific situation.

Conclusion

The modern leader operates in a dynamic and complex environment characterized by rapid technological change and evolving workforce expectations. A one-size-fits-all approach to management is no longer viable. Instead, leaders must be adaptable, agile, and able to leverage the strengths of different management theories.

By combining the efficiency and structure of classical management with the human-centric focus of human relations theory, and applying the flexibility of contingency management, leaders can create organizations that are both productive and people-oriented. As AI continues to evolve, the ability to balance human and technological factors will be critical for long-term success.

Ultimately, the most effective leaders will be those who can navigate this complex terrain by understanding the strengths and limitations of different management approaches and adapting their leadership style accordingly.

CHAPTER THREE

Intellect and Intelligence in Management Functions

Intellect and intelligence are often used interchangeably, but they carry distinct connotations in the realm of management. Intellect refers to the capacity for understanding and reasoning, while intelligence implies the practical application of knowledge and skills. In the context of management, both are essential for effective leadership and decision-making.

Intellect in Management Functions

Intellect, the raw cognitive power, underpins the ability to comprehend complex organizational issues and formulate strategies. It is the foundation upon which managerial skills are built.

- **Planning:** Intellect is essential for envisioning the future, setting goals, and developing strategic plans. It involves the ability to analyze market trends, assess organizational strengths and weaknesses, and identify opportunities and threats.

- **Organizing:** Intellect is crucial for designing organizational structures, allocating resources, and establishing effective communication channels. It requires the capacity to understand the interrelationships between different departments and functions and to create a coherent organizational framework.
- **Staffing:** Intellect plays a vital role in identifying talent, recruiting qualified employees, and developing their potential. It involves assessing job requirements, evaluating candidate qualifications, and matching individuals to appropriate roles.
- **Directing:** Intellect is necessary for effective leadership, motivation, and communication. It involves the ability to articulate goals, provide clear instructions, and inspire employees to achieve organizational objectives.
- **Controlling:** Intellect is essential for monitoring performance, measuring results, and taking corrective actions. It involves the ability to establish performance standards, collect and analyze data, and identify deviations from plans.

Intelligence in Management Functions

Intelligence goes beyond intellectual capacity and involves the practical application of knowledge and skills to achieve organizational goals. It is the ability to think critically, solve problems, and make sound decisions.

- **Planning:** Intelligence is crucial for converting strategic plans into actionable steps. It involves the ability to break down complex objectives into smaller, manageable tasks, and to allocate resources efficiently.

- **Organizing:** Intelligence is essential for implementing organizational structures and systems effectively. It involves the ability to adapt structures to changing conditions, resolve conflicts, and coordinate the activities of different departments.
- **Staffing:** Intelligence is necessary for building high-performing teams and developing employee talent. It involves the ability to identify training needs, provide mentorship, and create a positive work environment.
- **Directing:** Intelligence is crucial for motivating employees, resolving conflicts, and building strong relationships. It involves the ability to communicate effectively, provide feedback, and inspire trust.
- **Controlling:** Intelligence is essential for analyzing performance data, identifying root causes of problems, and implementing corrective actions. It involves the ability to make data-driven decisions and adapt to changing circumstances.

The Interplay of Intellect and Intelligence

Intellect and intelligence are interdependent. A high level of intellect without the ability to apply knowledge effectively may lead to impractical ideas. Conversely, strong intelligence without a solid intellectual foundation may result in short-term solutions and limited strategic thinking.

Successful managers possess a blend of both intellect and intelligence. They can think critically, analyze information, and develop innovative strategies. They can also implement these strategies effectively, motivate employees, and achieve organizational goals.

For example, a CEO with high intellect might develop a visionary strategy for the company. However, it is the CEO's intelligence that will determine how to execute the strategy, overcome challenges, and adapt to changing market conditions.

In conclusion, intellect and intelligence are both essential for effective management. Intellect provides the foundation for understanding and reasoning, while intelligence enables the practical application of knowledge and skills. By combining these two qualities, managers can make sound decisions, build high-performing teams, and achieve organizational success.

Adaptability: The Cornerstone of Corporate Resilience

Nature, in its infinite wisdom, offers a masterclass in adaptability. From the chameleon changing color to mimic its environment to the oak tree weathering storms, the natural world is a testament to the power of resilience. Similarly, in the corporate world, adaptability is not merely a desirable trait but a prerequisite for survival and growth.

The human mind, a marvel of evolution, possesses an innate capacity to learn, adapt, and innovate. We observe patterns, identify trends, and devise solutions to challenges, often drawing inspiration from the natural world around us. This ability to discern hidden opportunities within challenges is fundamental to human progress and, by extension, corporate success.

Consider the humble dandelion. Often dismissed as a weed, it exhibits extraordinary resilience, growing in the most inhospitable conditions. This unassuming plant offers a metaphor for businesses that thrive in adversity. It suggests a strategy of adaptability, resourcefulness, and the ability to find opportunities where others see obstacles.

However, while human ingenuity is invaluable, there are instances when external expertise is indispensable. Complex challenges often necessitate specialized knowledge and skills. This is where partnerships with consultants, experts, or other organizations become crucial. The ability to identify the appropriate external resources and effectively collaborate with them is a hallmark of adaptive leadership.

In essence, adaptability is a multifaceted skill that encompasses both internal capabilities and external partnerships. It requires a deep understanding of the environment, a willingness to experiment, and the ability to learn from both successes and failures. By cultivating a culture of adaptability, organizations can not only survive but thrive in an ever-changing business landscape.

This ability to seamlessly integrate internal strengths with external expertise is what truly distinguishes adaptable organizations. It is a dynamic interplay between human ingenuity and strategic partnerships that propels businesses forward.

CHAPTER FOUR

The Dual Role of Leadership: Prevention and Correction

A leader is akin to a physician, diagnosing the health of an organization, prescribing treatments, and ensuring overall well-being. This responsibility extends beyond simply addressing problems; it encompasses anticipating potential issues and preventing their occurrence. A leader who is adept at both preventive and corrective measures is instrumental in sustaining organizational health and growth.

The Importance of Prevention

Proactive leadership is essential in creating a resilient organization. Just as a healthy lifestyle prevents diseases, preventive measures in an organization can forestall crises. This involves a deep understanding of the organization's internal and external environment, identifying potential threats, and implementing strategies to mitigate them.

For example, a tech company might anticipate rapid technological advancements and invest in research and development to stay ahead of competitors. This preventive measure ensures the company remains innovative and relevant. Similarly, a retail company might conduct market research to predict consumer trends and adjust its product offerings accordingly, preventing sales decline.

Furthermore, fostering a strong organizational culture is a crucial preventive measure. A culture of open communication, trust, and employee empowerment can prevent issues like low morale, high turnover, and decreased productivity. Leaders who invest in employee well-being, provide opportunities for growth, and recognize achievements create a positive work environment that acts as a buffer against potential challenges.

The Art of Correction

While prevention is ideal, challenges inevitably arise. A leader's ability to respond effectively to crises is paramount. This requires a clear understanding of the problem, swift decision-making, and the ability to implement corrective actions.

Consider a manufacturing company facing a product recall due to a quality issue. A strong leader will swiftly initiate a recall, investigate the root cause, implement corrective actions to prevent recurrence, and communicate transparently with customers and stakeholders. This demonstrates the importance of a rapid and decisive response to a crisis.

Another example is a company experiencing declining sales. A leader might analyze market trends, competitor actions, and internal factors to identify the root cause. Corrective actions could include restructuring sales teams, launching new products, or cutting costs. Effective leadership in this situation involves not only addressing the immediate problem but also implementing strategies to prevent future declines.

The Interplay of Prevention and Correction

It's essential to recognize that prevention and correction are interconnected. Preventive measures can reduce the likelihood of crises but do not eliminate them entirely. Conversely, effective corrective actions can provide valuable insights for enhancing preventive strategies.

For instance, a company that successfully manages a product recall might implement stricter quality control measures to prevent future incidents. This is an example of using a corrective action to improve preventive practices. Similarly, a company that overcomes a financial crisis might establish more robust financial controls to prevent similar issues in the future.

The Leader as a Visionary and Problem-Solver

A successful leader is both a visionary and a problem-solver. They must be able to anticipate future challenges and develop strategies to address them while also being prepared to respond effectively to unexpected crises. This requires a combination of strategic thinking, adaptability, and decisiveness.

By mastering the art of both prevention and correction, leaders can create organizations that are not only resilient but also thrive in a dynamic and competitive environment. It is through this balanced approach that leaders can inspire confidence, build trust, and achieve long-term success.

In conclusion, a leader's ability to effectively balance preventive and corrective measures is crucial for organizational health and success. By anticipating challenges, implementing proactive strategies, and responding decisively to crises, leaders can create a sustainable and thriving organization.

CHAPTER FIVE

Organizational Setbacks: Internal and External Challenges

Just as individuals experience unexpected health issues despite their best efforts, organizations can encounter setbacks regardless of meticulous planning and execution. These setbacks can be categorized into two primary types: internal and external.

Internal Setbacks

Internal factors are those within an organization's control, and while they can often be mitigated through effective management, they can still lead to significant challenges.

- **Leadership Challenges:** Ineffective leadership, poor decision-making, or a lack of strategic vision can hinder an organization's progress. For instance, a CEO's inability to adapt to changing market conditions can lead to missed opportunities and financial losses.
- **Organizational Culture Issues:** A toxic work environment characterized by low morale, lack of

collaboration, or high turnover can negatively impact productivity, innovation, and employee retention.

- **Operational Inefficiencies:** Poor processes, systems failures, or supply chain disruptions can disrupt operations, leading to financial losses and customer dissatisfaction. For example, a manufacturing company experiencing frequent equipment breakdowns can result in production delays and increased costs.
- **Financial Mismanagement:** Ineffective financial planning, budgeting, or control can lead to cash flow problems, insolvency, or missed investment opportunities.
- **Human Capital Issues:** Talent shortages, skill gaps, or employee dissatisfaction can impact organizational performance. A lack of qualified personnel in key roles can hinder growth and innovation.

External Setbacks

External factors are beyond an organization's direct control and can significantly impact its operations.

- **Economic Conditions:** Economic downturns, recessions, or inflation can reduce consumer spending, increase costs, and decrease profitability. For example, a decline in consumer confidence during a recession can lead to decreased sales for retailers.
- **Industry Changes:** Technological advancements, shifts in consumer preferences, or increased competition can disrupt established business models. The rise of e-commerce, for instance, has significantly impacted traditional brick-and-mortar retailers.
- **Regulatory Changes:** New or modified government regulations can increase costs, limit business operations,

or create competitive disadvantages. For example, stricter environmental regulations can lead to increased compliance expenses for manufacturing companies.

- **Natural Disasters:** Natural calamities such as earthquakes, hurricanes, or floods can cause significant damage to property, disrupt supply chains, and lead to business interruptions.
- **Geopolitical Events:** Wars, political instability, or trade disputes can impact global supply chains, increase costs, and create uncertainty for businesses.

It is essential to note that while leaders cannot control external factors, they can develop strategies to mitigate their impact. For instance, during an economic downturn, a company might focus on cost reduction, product innovation, and market diversification. Similarly, in the face of regulatory changes, a company can invest in compliance expertise and explore opportunities to leverage new regulations as a competitive advantage.

Ultimately, effective leadership involves a combination of foresight, adaptability, and resilience to navigate both internal and external challenges. By understanding the potential sources of setbacks and developing appropriate response plans, leaders can increase their organization's chances of success.

While it is impossible to eliminate all risks, a proactive approach to identifying and addressing potential challenges can significantly enhance an organization's ability to weather storms and emerge stronger.

Section 2: Tools and Techniques for Effective Management

1. The Role of Relevant Information in Efficient Contingency Management
2. The Power of Lateral Thinking in Leadership and Investigations
3. Integrating Lateral Thinking into Organizations
4. Crisis Management: Investigating the Storm

The Role of Relevant Information in Efficient Contingency Management

Contingency management, the art of planning for unforeseen circumstances, is a cornerstone of effective leadership. However, its efficacy hinges on the quality and timeliness of the information available to decision-makers. Relevant information is the lifeblood of contingency planning, enabling organizations to anticipate risks, develop robust strategies, and respond effectively to crises.

The Nature of Relevant Information

Relevant information is data that is pertinent to a specific situation, accurate, timely, and actionable. It should provide insights into potential risks, vulnerabilities, and opportunities. This information can be derived from various sources, including:

- **Internal Data:** Financial reports, operational metrics, employee surveys, and customer feedback can provide valuable insights into an organization's strengths, weaknesses, and potential vulnerabilities.

- **External Data:** Market research, economic indicators, industry trends, and competitor analysis offer a broader perspective on the external environment and potential threats.
- **Expert Opinions:** Insights from industry experts, consultants, and subject matter experts can provide valuable perspectives on potential risks and mitigation strategies.
- **Historical Data:** Past incidents, near-misses, and successful crisis responses can offer valuable lessons for future contingency planning.

The Role of Information in Contingency Planning

Relevant information plays a crucial role in several stages of contingency management:

- **Risk Identification:** By analyzing data from various sources, organizations can identify potential threats and vulnerabilities. For example, a retail company might use sales data to identify product lines with declining sales, which could indicate potential risks to revenue.
- **Risk Assessment:** Information is essential for evaluating the potential impact and likelihood of identified risks. By quantifying the potential consequences of different scenarios, organizations can prioritize risks and allocate resources accordingly.
- **Contingency Plan Development:** Information is used to develop specific plans for addressing identified risks. For example, a manufacturing company might use supply chain data to develop contingency plans for disruptions in raw material supply.

- **Crisis Response:** During a crisis, timely and accurate information is crucial for making effective decisions. For example, a financial institution experiencing a cyberattack would need real-time information on the extent of the breach, customer impact, and available resources to respond effectively.
- **Post-Incident Analysis:** Information collected during and after a crisis is essential for learning from the experience and improving future contingency plans. For example, a company that experiences a product recall can use data on customer complaints and product defects to identify root causes and prevent similar incidents.

Challenges in Information Management

While relevant information is essential for effective contingency management, several challenges can hinder its acquisition and utilization:

- **Information Overload:** The abundance of data can overwhelm decision-makers, making it difficult to identify critical information.
- **Data Quality:** Inaccurate or incomplete data can lead to flawed decision-making.
- **Data Sharing:** Silos within organizations can prevent the effective sharing of information across departments, hindering contingency planning.
- **Real-time Access:** The ability to access and analyze information in real-time is crucial during a crisis, but technological limitations can pose challenges.

Overcoming Challenges and Maximizing Information Value

To overcome these challenges, organizations should invest in data management systems, data quality initiatives, and employee training. Additionally, fostering a culture of information sharing and collaboration is essential.

Furthermore, organizations should prioritize the development of early warning systems that can detect potential crises before they occur. This requires continuous monitoring of both internal and external data sources and the ability to identify patterns and anomalies.

By effectively managing information, organizations can enhance their ability to anticipate risks, develop robust contingency plans, and respond effectively to crises. In today's complex and rapidly changing business environment, the role of relevant information in contingency management cannot be overstated.

CHAPTER SEVEN

The Power of Lateral Thinking in Leadership and Investigations

Lateral thinking, a cognitive process that involves exploring multiple possibilities and challenging assumptions, is a critical skill for both leaders and investigators. It is the ability to think creatively and unconventionally, often leading to innovative solutions and breakthroughs.

Lateral Thinking in Leadership

Effective leadership requires the ability to address complex challenges and make sound decisions. Lateral thinking empowers leaders to:

- **Foster Innovation:** By encouraging unconventional thinking, leaders can create a culture of innovation where new ideas and approaches are valued.
- **Solve Complex Problems:** When faced with challenges, lateral thinking allows leaders to explore alternative perspectives and find creative solutions.
- **Make Better Decisions:** By considering multiple possibilities, leaders can reduce the risk of making hasty

or suboptimal decisions.
- **Improve Problem-Solving:** Lateral thinking helps leaders to identify root causes of problems rather than simply addressing symptoms.
- **Build High-Performing Teams:** Leaders who encourage lateral thinking can foster a team environment where everyone feels empowered to contribute ideas.

For example, a company facing declining sales might traditionally focus on reducing costs or increasing advertising. A leader with lateral thinking skills might question the core product or target market, leading to the development of a new product line or a shift in customer focus.

Lateral Thinking in Investigations

In the realm of investigations, lateral thinking is essential for uncovering hidden truths and solving complex cases. It allows investigators to:

- **Identify New Leads:** By challenging assumptions and exploring alternative theories, investigators can uncover new leads that might otherwise be overlooked.
- **Develop Creative Investigative Techniques:** Lateral thinking can lead to the development of innovative investigative methods and tools.
- **Overcome Obstacles:** When faced with dead ends, lateral thinking can help investigators find new ways to approach the case.
- **Analyze Information Differently:** By looking at information from different perspectives, investigators can uncover hidden patterns and connections.
- **Think Outside the Box:** In cases of complex fraud or white-collar crime, lateral thinking is often required to

identify the perpetrators and their methods.

For example, an investigator looking into a case of employee theft might traditionally focus on analyzing financial records and conducting employee interviews. A lateral thinker might consider examining the company's security systems, employee turnover rates, or even the company's organizational structure for clues.

CHAPTER EIGHT

Integrating Lateral Thinking into Organizations

To foster lateral thinking, organizations should:

- **Encourage Open-Mindedness:** Create a culture where employees feel comfortable challenging the status quo and expressing unconventional ideas.
- **Provide Training:** Offer training programs in creativity and problem-solving techniques.
- **Reward Innovation:** Recognize and reward employees for innovative ideas and solutions.
- **Create Cross-Functional Teams:** Bring together people from different departments to encourage diverse perspectives.
- **Promote Experimentation:** Encourage employees to experiment with new ideas and approaches.

By incorporating lateral thinking into their leadership and investigative practices, organizations can enhance their problem-solving abilities, foster innovation, and achieve greater success.

Due diligence is a comprehensive investigation or audit of a potential investment or business transaction. It's a critical step before merging, acquiring, or partnering with another company to identify potential risks and opportunities.

Key Areas of Due Diligence

1. **Financial Due Diligence:**

   - **Financial Statements Analysis:** Scrutinizing income statements, balance sheets, and cash flow statements for accuracy, consistency, and anomalies.
   - **Revenue and Expense Analysis:** Examining revenue streams, cost structures, and profitability trends.
   - **Tax Compliance:** Assessing tax returns, audits, and potential tax liabilities.
   - **Debt Analysis:** Evaluating the company's debt structure, interest rates, and repayment capacity.
   - **Working Capital Management:** Analyzing the company's ability to manage its short-term assets and liabilities.

2. **Legal Due Diligence:**

   - **Contract Review:** Examining contracts with customers, suppliers, employees, and partners for potential liabilities.
   - **Intellectual Property Assessment:** Evaluating the strength and protection of patents, trademarks, and copyrights.
   - **Regulatory Compliance:** Assessing the company's adherence to industry regulations and

environmental laws.

- **Litigation Analysis:** Identifying ongoing or potential legal disputes.

3. **Operational Due Diligence:**

- **Business Model Analysis:** Evaluating the company's business model, revenue generation, and cost structure.
- **Supply Chain Assessment:** Examining the company's supply chain for risks, dependencies, and potential disruptions.
- **Operational Efficiency:** Analyzing the company's production processes, quality control, and logistics.
- **Human Resources Evaluation:** Assessing employee morale, turnover rates, and potential labor issues.

4. **Strategic Due Diligence:**

- **Market Analysis:** Evaluating the company's market position, competitive landscape, and growth opportunities.
- **Customer Analysis:** Understanding customer demographics, preferences, and loyalty.
- **Technology Assessment:** Evaluating the company's IT infrastructure, systems, and data security.

Talent Poaching: A Silent Corporate Threat

Talent poaching, the practice of luring away employees from rival companies, has become a contentious yet prevalent strategy in the corporate world.

While it can be seen as a testament to an organization's attractiveness, it also poses significant challenges to the competitive landscape.

Understanding Talent Poaching

Talent poaching occurs when a company actively recruits employees from a competitor, often targeting individuals with specialized skills or knowledge. This practice can be driven by various factors, including a shortage of skilled talent, the desire to gain a competitive advantage, or the need to fill critical roles quickly.

The Impact of Talent Poaching

The consequences of talent poaching can be far-reaching. For the losing company, it can lead to:

- **Loss of Intellectual Property:** Employees often carry valuable knowledge and trade secrets with them.
- **Disruption of Operations:** The departure of key personnel can disrupt ongoing projects and negatively impact productivity.
- **Increased Recruitment and Training Costs:** Replacing poached employees requires time and resources.
- **Damaged Morale:** The departure of valued employees can impact the morale of remaining staff.

For the gaining company, while the acquisition of top talent can be beneficial, it also carries risks:

- **Integration Challenges:** Integrating new hires into the company culture and workflow can be difficult.
- **Legal and Ethical Concerns:** Aggressive poaching tactics can damage a company's reputation.
- **Dependency on Poached Talent:** Overreliance on poached employees can create long-term vulnerabilities.

Defending Against Talent Poaching

To protect against talent poaching, organizations can implement the following strategies:

- **Employee Engagement:** Foster a positive work environment to increase employee satisfaction and loyalty.
- **Competitive Compensation:** Offer competitive salaries and benefits packages.
- **Career Development:** Provide opportunities for growth and advancement.
- **Intellectual Property Protection:** Safeguard sensitive information through legal and technical measures.

- **Employee Non-Compete Agreements:** Carefully draft and enforce non-compete agreements.
- **Early Warning Systems:** Monitor employee sentiment and identify potential departure risks.

By adopting a proactive approach to talent management, companies can significantly reduce their vulnerability to poaching and build a more resilient workforce.

The Ethical Debate

Talent poaching raises ethical questions about fair competition and the treatment of employees. While it is legal to recruit employees from other companies, aggressive tactics and unethical behavior can damage an organization's reputation. Striking a balance between protecting one's interests and maintaining ethical standards is crucial in today's competitive business environment.

Talent poaching is a complex issue with far-reaching implications. By understanding the challenges and implementing effective strategies, organizations can mitigate its impact and protect their valuable human capital.

CHAPTER TEN

Crisis Management: Investigating the Storm

Crisis management is the process of anticipating, preventing, mitigating, and responding to crises. In today's hyper-connected world, crises can erupt rapidly, with potentially devastating consequences for a company's reputation, finances, and operations. Effective crisis management necessitates swift and thorough investigations to understand the root cause, contain the damage, and prevent recurrence.

Types of Crises

- **Data Breaches:** Unauthorized access to sensitive information can lead to significant financial losses, reputational damage, and legal liabilities.
- **Product Recalls:** Defective or harmful products can result in injuries, deaths, and widespread public outcry.
- **Public Relations Disasters:** Negative publicity, social media backlash, or executive misconduct can erode trust and damage a company's brand.

The Role of Investigations

Investigations are crucial in understanding the full extent of a crisis, identifying its root causes, and developing effective response strategies.

- **Data Breaches:** Investigations focus on determining the nature and scope of the breach, identifying the compromised data, and understanding how the breach occurred. Digital forensics is essential to gather evidence and trace the attack. For example, the Equifax data breach exposed sensitive personal information of millions of consumers, necessitating a comprehensive investigation to understand the vulnerabilities and prevent future incidents.
- **Product Recalls:** Investigations aim to identify the cause of the product defect, determine the extent of the problem, and develop a recall strategy. Product testing, supply chain analysis, and consumer complaints are key components of these investigations. The Toyota accelerator pedal recall is a prime example of a well-managed product recall, involving a thorough investigation to identify the root cause of the problem.
- **Public Relations Disasters:** Investigations focus on understanding the origin of the crisis, assessing its impact on the company's reputation, and identifying the stakeholders affected. Social media monitoring, media analysis, and employee interviews can provide valuable insights. The United Airlines passenger dragging incident is a stark example of a public relations disaster that required a swift and comprehensive investigation to restore public trust.

Key Investigation Steps

1. **Rapid Response:** Assemble a crisis management team to initiate the investigation promptly.
2. **Evidence Collection:** Gather relevant data, documents, and witness statements.
3. **Root Cause Analysis:** Identify the underlying factors that contributed to the crisis.
4. **Impact Assessment:** Evaluate the extent of the damage to the company's reputation, finances, and operations.
5. **Stakeholder Analysis:** Identify key stakeholders and assess their concerns.
6. **Communication Strategy:** Develop a clear and consistent communication plan to address stakeholders' concerns.
7. **Corrective Actions:** Implement measures to prevent similar crises in the future.

Challenges and Best Practices

Investigating crises can be complex and emotionally charged. Key challenges include:

- **Time Pressure:** The need to respond quickly often limits the time available for investigation.
- **Information Overload:** Managing vast amounts of data can be overwhelming.
- **Stakeholder Management:** Balancing the interests of various stakeholders can be difficult.

To overcome these challenges, organizations should:

- Develop a crisis management plan in advance.
- Establish clear roles and responsibilities for the crisis management team.

- Utilize technology to facilitate data collection and analysis.
- Train employees in crisis response procedures.
- Conduct regular crisis simulations to test response plans.

By effectively managing crises through thorough investigations and timely responses, organizations can protect their reputation, minimize financial losses, and build trust with stakeholders.

Section 3: Investigative Techniques and Corporate Security

1. The Role of Private Investigators in Management
2. The Role of Private Investigators in Various Contingencies
3. Corporate Investigations: A Deeper Dive with Indian Case Studies
4. Undercover Operations: A Double-Edged Sword
5. Undercover Operations in the Healthcare Industry
6. Undercover Operations in Corporate Investigations
7. The Undercover Operation and Entrapment
8. Surveillance: A Double-Edged Sword
9. Challenges in Implementing Surveillance Programs
10. Surveillance in the IT Industry
11. Surveillance in the Manufacturing Industry
12. Surveillance Technologies in Manufacturing
13. Video Analytics: The Intelligence Behind the Camera
14. Challenges in Implementing Surveillance Systems
15. Overcoming the Challenge of False Positives in Surveillance Systems
16. False Positives in the Financial Industry
17. False Positives in Healthcare: A Complex Challenge
18. False Positives in Cybersecurity

The Role of Private Investigators in Management

The role of a private investigator (PI) in management is often underestimated, yet it's becoming increasingly crucial in today's complex business environment. They serve as an essential component of a company's risk management strategy, providing a unique perspective and skill set that complements internal resources.

The Investigator as a Risk Mitigation Tool

- **Due Diligence Investigations:** Before significant business decisions, such as mergers, acquisitions, or partnerships, PIs conduct thorough background checks on potential partners. They uncover financial irregularities, legal issues, or reputational risks that could impact the deal.
- **Fraud Prevention:** Private investigators can identify potential fraud within an organization by conducting internal investigations, analyzing financial data, and interviewing employees. They can detect discrepancies,

anomalies, and red flags indicative of fraudulent activities.

- **Asset Protection:** Protecting intellectual property, trade secrets, and other valuable assets is crucial for businesses. PIs can conduct investigations to identify potential threats, such as industrial espionage or counterfeit products.
- **Employee Investigations:** PIs can investigate allegations of misconduct, such as theft, fraud, or discrimination. They gather evidence and conduct interviews to build a case, protecting the company's reputation and ensuring a fair investigation.

The Investigator as a Strategic Partner

- **Competitive Intelligence:** Understanding the competitive landscape is essential for business success. PIs can gather information on competitors' strategies, products, and market share to inform strategic decision-making.
- **Crisis Management:** In the event of a crisis, such as a product recall or data breach, PIs can assist in damage control by gathering information, conducting investigations, and communicating with stakeholders.
- **Background Checks:** Hiring the right employees is crucial for organizational success. PIs conduct comprehensive background checks to verify employment history, education, criminal records, and other relevant information.
- **Loss Prevention:** PIs can identify vulnerabilities in security systems and procedures, helping to prevent theft, vandalism, and other losses.

The Investigator as an Information Gatherer

- **Data Collection:** PIs are skilled at gathering information from various sources, including public records, social media, and confidential databases. They use their investigative skills to uncover hidden information that might be relevant to a case.
- **Surveillance:** In certain cases, surveillance may be necessary to gather evidence or verify information. PIs are trained in surveillance techniques and can collect visual and audio evidence.
- **Interviewing and Interrogation:** PIs are experts in conducting interviews and interrogations. They can obtain information from witnesses, suspects, and other relevant parties.

Challenges and Considerations

While private investigators offer valuable services, it's essential to consider the ethical implications and legal boundaries of their work. Companies must ensure that investigators adhere to relevant laws and regulations. Additionally, the cost of hiring a private investigator can be significant, and it's essential to weigh the potential benefits against the costs.

In conclusion, private investigators play a multifaceted role in modern management. By leveraging their skills in investigation, data collection, and analysis, they can help organizations mitigate risks, protect assets, and make informed decisions. As the business landscape becomes increasingly complex, the demand for their services is likely to grow.

CHAPTER TWELVE

The Role of Private Investigators in Various Contingencies

Preventive Investigations

Due Diligence: Before entering into significant business partnerships or acquisitions, private investigators conduct comprehensive background checks on potential partners. This includes financial investigations, legal checks, and reputation analysis. For example, a company considering a merger might engage a PI to verify the financial health of the target company and identify any potential liabilities.

Open Media/Social Media Checks: PIs monitor public records, news articles, and social media platforms for information relevant to an individual or organization. This can help identify potential risks or opportunities. For instance, a company hiring a high-profile executive might use social media checks to assess the individual's online reputation and potential liabilities.

Vetting: PIs conduct thorough background checks on individuals, such as employees, contractors, or business partners. This includes verifying employment history, education, criminal records, and financial stability. For example, a law firm might use PI services to vet potential new hires to ensure they have the necessary qualifications and no criminal history.

Security Risk Assessment: PIs evaluate an organization's security vulnerabilities by conducting physical site surveys, assessing access control systems, and identifying potential threats. For instance, a retail company might engage a PI to assess the security of its stores and warehouses to prevent theft and loss.

Insurance Investigations

Motor OD Claims: In cases of suspected fraud or exaggeration in motor vehicle accident claims, PIs investigate the circumstances surrounding the accident, the extent of injuries, and the claimant's activities. This helps insurance companies prevent fraudulent payouts. For example, a PI might investigate a claim of whiplash by conducting surveillance on the claimant to determine their actual level of mobility.

Non-Motor Claims: PIs investigate claims related to property damage, theft, or personal injury. They gather evidence, interview witnesses, and analyze documentation to assess the validity of claims. For instance, a home insurance company might engage a PI to investigate a fire claim to determine the cause of the fire and whether there was any intentional wrongdoing.

Third-Party Claims: PIs investigate claims involving multiple parties to determine liability and damages. For example, in a car accident involving multiple vehicles, a PI might investigate the actions of each driver to determine fault.

Recovery Assistance: PIs assist insurance companies in recovering funds from fraudulent or exaggerated claims.

They gather evidence and build cases to support legal action. For example, a PI might investigate a claim of stolen jewelry and recover the stolen items through surveillance and investigation.

Corporate Investigations

Assess Internal Issues: PIs investigate allegations of fraud, theft, or other misconduct within an organization. They conduct interviews, review documents, and gather evidence to build a case. For instance, a company might engage a PI to investigate suspected employee theft.

Background Checks: PIs conduct pre-employment background checks to verify information provided by job applicants. This helps companies hire trustworthy and qualified employees. For example, a financial institution might use PI services to verify the employment history and criminal records of potential employees.

Dual Employment Check: PIs verify if an employee is holding multiple jobs without the knowledge of their primary employer. This helps prevent conflicts of interest and ensures employee loyalty. For example, a healthcare facility might use PI services to check if a nurse is working at multiple hospitals.

Essential Mergers & Acquisitions Support Services: PIs provide due diligence support, asset tracing, and fraud prevention services during mergers and acquisitions. For example, a company acquiring another company might engage a PI to investigate potential liabilities and identify hidden assets.

Litigation Support Services: PIs gather evidence, interview witnesses, and conduct surveillance to support legal proceedings. They provide crucial information to attorneys and help build strong cases. For example, a law firm might engage a PI to gather evidence for a personal injury case.

In conclusion, private investigators play a critical role in various aspects of business operations. By providing investigative services, they help organizations mitigate risks, prevent fraud, protect assets, and make informed decisions.

CHAPTER THIRTEEN

Corporate Investigations: A Deeper Dive with Indian Case Studies

Corporate investigations are critical for maintaining organizational integrity and protecting shareholder value. In India, several high-profile cases have underscored the importance of robust investigative practices.

Types of Corporate Investigations

Before delving into case studies, it's essential to understand the broad spectrum of corporate investigations:

- **Financial Fraud:** This includes embezzlement, bribery, corruption, and accounting irregularities.
- **Intellectual Property Theft:** Protecting trade secrets, patents, and copyrights is crucial. Investigations focus on identifying and preventing theft.
- **Employee Misconduct:** Issues like theft, fraud, discrimination, harassment, or substance abuse can damage a company's reputation.

- **Due Diligence:** Before mergers, acquisitions, or partnerships, investigations assess the target company's financial health, legal liabilities, and operational risks.
- **Internal Controls Assessment:** Evaluating internal processes and controls to identify vulnerabilities and prevent fraud.
- **Crisis Management:** Responding to crises like data breaches, product recalls, or public relations disasters requires swift and effective investigations.

High-Profile Indian Cases

India has witnessed several corporate scandals that highlight the need for robust investigative practices.

- **Satyam Computer Services:** One of the most infamous cases, Satyam involved a massive accounting fraud where the company inflated its revenue and assets. The scandal led to the arrest of the company's founder and exposed the weaknesses in India's corporate governance framework.
- **2G Spectrum Scam:** This high-profile case involved alleged irregularities in the allocation of 2G spectrum licenses to telecom companies. The investigation revealed significant financial losses to the government and led to the conviction of several high-profile individuals.
- **Coal Scam:** The allocation of coal blocks to companies without proper bidding processes resulted in substantial losses to the public exchequer. Investigations into the scam exposed the nexus between politicians, bureaucrats, and corporate entities.

The Role of Private Investigators

Private investigators play a crucial role in corporate investigations by providing specialized skills and resources. Their involvement can include:

- **Evidence Collection:** Gathering documents, electronic data, and witness statements.
- **Surveillance:** Monitoring individuals or locations to gather evidence of misconduct or illegal activities.
- **Undercover Operations:** Posing as potential customers or employees to uncover fraudulent activities.
- **Financial Analysis:** Investigating financial records for anomalies and red flags.
- **Background Checks:** Verifying the credentials and backgrounds of employees, contractors, or business partners.

Challenges and Best Practices

Corporate investigations can be complex and sensitive, requiring careful planning and execution. Challenges include:

- **Preserving Evidence:** Ensuring the integrity of evidence is crucial. Proper chain of custody and handling procedures are essential.
- **Maintaining Confidentiality:** Protecting sensitive information is critical to prevent leaks and damage to reputations.
- **Legal and Ethical Compliance:** Adhering to laws and regulations is essential to avoid legal repercussions.

To mitigate these challenges, organizations should:

- Develop clear investigation protocols and procedures.

- Establish a dedicated investigations team or outsource to specialized firms.
- Conduct regular training for employees on fraud prevention and detection.
- Foster a culture of ethical behavior and whistleblowing.

By implementing robust investigative practices, companies can protect their reputation, minimize financial losses, and maintain the trust of stakeholders.

CHAPTER FOURTEEN

Undercover Operations: A Double-Edged Sword

Undercover operations, a clandestine investigative technique, involve agents assuming false identities to infiltrate organizations or groups to gather intelligence. While controversial, they can be highly effective in uncovering fraudulent activities, especially when conventional methods fall short.

Types of Undercover Operations

- **Customer Undercover:** An investigator poses as a potential customer to expose fraudulent practices, such as price gouging, product tampering, or false advertising. For instance, an undercover investigator might visit a car dealership to check for deceptive sales tactics or hidden fees.

- **Employee Undercover:** Infiltrating an organization as a new employee allows investigators to observe internal operations, identify potential fraud, or uncover theft. For example, an undercover investigator might be placed in a warehouse to investigate inventory discrepancies.

- **Mystery Shopper:** While not strictly undercover, mystery shopping involves posing as a customer to assess service quality, compliance with regulations, and identify fraudulent activities.

Challenges and Considerations

Undercover operations are complex and fraught with risks. Key challenges include:

- **Legal and Ethical Implications:** Undercover work must adhere to strict legal and ethical guidelines to avoid compromising evidence or violating individual rights.
- **Operational Risks:** Agents face potential danger, stress, and the risk of being discovered.
- **Evidence Admissibility:** Ensuring that evidence collected through undercover operations is admissible in court is crucial.
- **Cost and Resources:** Undercover operations can be expensive and time-consuming, requiring significant resources.
- **Ethical Dilemmas:** Agents may face moral dilemmas when confronted with illegal or unethical activities.

Case Studies

- **Insurance Fraud:** Undercover investigators have been used to expose staged accidents, fraudulent claims, and organized crime rings involved in insurance fraud. By posing as potential customers or witnesses, investigators can gather evidence to support legal action.

- **Counterfeit Goods:** Undercover operations have helped dismantle counterfeit product networks. By purchasing counterfeit goods, investigators can trace the supply chain and identify the source of the illegal products.
- **Corporate Espionage:** In cases of suspected industrial espionage, undercover investigators may infiltrate rival companies to uncover trade secret theft or other illicit activities.

Balancing Act

Undercover operations are a powerful tool, but they should be used judiciously and in conjunction with other investigative methods. It's essential to weigh the potential benefits against the risks and to ensure that all legal and ethical guidelines are followed.

By carefully planning and executing undercover operations, organizations can effectively combat fraud, protect their assets, and maintain their reputation.

CHAPTER FIFTEEN

Undercover Operations in the Healthcare Industry

The healthcare industry, characterized by complex billing systems, high-value services, and vulnerable patients, is a fertile ground for fraud. Undercover operations have proven to be particularly effective in uncovering a range of illicit activities within this sector.

Common Healthcare Frauds

- **Medicare and Medicaid Fraud:** This encompasses a wide range of schemes, including billing for services not rendered, upcoding (billing for more expensive services), and patient identity theft.
- **Insurance Fraud:** This involves submitting false or exaggerated claims for medical treatments or procedures.
- **Prescription Drug Fraud:** This includes illegal prescription drug manufacturing, distribution, and diversion.

Role of Undercover Operations

- **Patient Identity Theft:** Undercover investigators can pose as patients to identify clinics or doctors involved in patient identity theft for fraudulent billing purposes.
- **Phantom Billing:** By posing as patients or insurance representatives, investigators can uncover instances of billing for services that were never provided.
- **Prescription Drug Diversion:** Undercover operations can be used to infiltrate illegal drug distribution networks, identifying sources of diverted prescription medications.
- **Kickbacks and Bribery:** By posing as medical providers or pharmaceutical representatives, investigators can uncover schemes involving kickbacks or bribes for patient referrals.

Challenges and Considerations

- **Patient Privacy:** Undercover operations must be conducted with utmost care to protect patient privacy and confidentiality.
- **Legal and Ethical Implications:** Adhering to healthcare regulations and ethical guidelines is crucial.
- **Safety Risks:** Undercover agents may face risks of exposure or retaliation.

Case Studies

While specific cases often remain confidential, numerous high-profile investigations have exposed significant healthcare fraud. For instance, undercover operations have led to the dismantling of organized crime rings involved in prescription drug trafficking, the arrest of doctors and clinic owners for fraudulent billing, and the recovery of millions of dollars in lost funds.

Conclusion

Undercover operations in the healthcare industry are a powerful tool in combating fraud. By exposing illegal activities and bringing perpetrators to justice, these investigations protect patients, insurers, and taxpayers. However, they must be conducted carefully, with a strong emphasis on legal and ethical considerations

A Clarification on Covert Operations in Corporate Management

Before we delve into specific types, it's crucial to clarify that the term "covert operations" in a corporate context typically refers to *investigative* or *intelligence-gathering* activities rather than clandestine actions associated with espionage or espionage-like activities.

While the term might seem dramatic, it accurately reflects the need for discretion and secrecy often required in these corporate functions.

Types of Covert Operations in Corporate Management

1. **Undercover Investigations:**

   - **Employee Misconduct:** Posing as employees or customers to uncover theft, fraud, or other misconduct.
   - **Industrial Espionage:** Investigating suspected theft of trade secrets or intellectual property.
   - **Supply Chain Verification:** Undercover agents can verify the authenticity of products, working

conditions, and ethical sourcing practices.

2. **Surveillance:**

    ◦ **Employee Activity:** Monitoring employee behavior to detect potential misconduct or security breaches.
    ◦ **Competitor Analysis:** Observing competitors' operations to gather information on their strategies and tactics.
    ◦ **Asset Protection:** Protecting physical assets through surveillance to deter theft or vandalism.

3. **Information Gathering:**

    ◦ **Open-Source Intelligence (OSINT):** Collecting publicly available information from various sources to build a comprehensive picture of a situation or individual.
    ◦ **Human Intelligence (HUMINT):** Gathering information through direct interaction with people, often using undercover methods.
    ◦ **Database Searches:** Accessing public and private databases to find relevant information.

4. **Digital Forensics:**

    ◦ **Data Recovery:** Retrieving deleted or corrupted data from electronic devices.
    ◦ **E-Discovery:** Identifying and collecting electronically stored information for legal proceedings.
    ◦ **Cybersecurity Investigations:** Investigating cyberattacks and data breaches.

Ethical Considerations and Legal Implications

It's essential to conduct covert operations within legal and ethical boundaries. Key considerations include:

- **Privacy Laws:** Adhering to data protection and privacy regulations.
- **Employee Rights:** Respecting employee rights and avoiding illegal surveillance.
- **Corporate Ethics:** Maintaining ethical standards and avoiding unethical practices.
- **Legal Counsel:** Consulting with legal experts to ensure compliance with all applicable laws.

A Note on Terminology

While the term "covert operations" might be used in a corporate context, it's essential to distinguish these activities from the clandestine operations often associated with government intelligence agencies. Corporate investigations primarily focus on gathering information and evidence for legal or business purposes, rather than engaging in espionage or sabotage.

By understanding the types of covert operations and their potential applications, businesses can better protect their assets, mitigate risks, and make informed decisions.

CHAPTER SIXTEEN

Undercover Operations in Corporate Investigations

Undercover operations are a specialized investigative technique employed by organizations to uncover hidden issues, protect assets, and maintain operational integrity. While often associated with law enforcement, these methods have become increasingly prevalent in the corporate world.

Investigation of Employee Misconduct

Employee misconduct, ranging from theft and fraud to sabotage and data breaches, can inflict significant damage on a company. Undercover operations offer a unique perspective into the internal workings of an organization.

- **Undercover Employees:** By infiltrating the workforce as a regular employee, investigators can observe firsthand activities, identify potential red flags, and gather evidence of misconduct. This approach can be particularly effective in uncovering theft, fraud, or drug use within the workplace.

- **Mystery Shoppers:** While not strictly undercover, mystery shopping can reveal employee misconduct related to customer service, sales practices, or compliance with company policies.

Challenges and Considerations:

- **Ethical Implications:** Undercover operations raise ethical concerns about employee privacy and the potential for creating a hostile work environment.
- **Legal Considerations:** Adherence to labor laws and privacy regulations is crucial.
- **Evidence Admissibility:** Ensuring that evidence collected through undercover operations is admissible in court requires careful planning and documentation.
- **Operational Risks:** Undercover employees face potential risks, such as exposure or retaliation.

Industrial Espionage

The theft of trade secrets, intellectual property, and confidential information can have devastating consequences for a company. Undercover operations can play a vital role in identifying and preventing such activities.

- **Undercover Employees:** By infiltrating competing organizations, investigators can uncover the extent of trade secret theft, identify the individuals involved, and gather evidence to support legal action.
- **Supply Chain Investigations:** Undercover operations can be used to verify the authenticity of products and identify counterfeit goods, which can protect a company's brand reputation and intellectual property.

Challenges and Considerations:

- **Counterintelligence:** Protecting the investigator's identity and preventing counter-surveillance is paramount.
- **Legal Risks:** Operating in a competitive environment requires careful consideration of anti-competitive practices and trade secret laws.
- **Ethical Dilemmas:** Undercover employees may face moral challenges when confronted with illegal or unethical activities.

Supply Chain Verification

Ensuring the integrity of the supply chain is essential for maintaining product quality, protecting brand reputation, and complying with ethical and legal standards. Undercover operations can be used to verify various aspects of the supply chain.

- **Factory Audits:** Undercover investigators can pose as quality control inspectors to assess working conditions, labor practices, and product quality.
- **Product Authenticity:** By purchasing products from different sources, investigators can verify the authenticity of goods and identify counterfeit items.
- **Ethical Sourcing:** Undercover operations can help ensure compliance with environmental and social standards throughout the supply chain.

Challenges and Considerations:

- **Global Supply Chains:** Investigating complex global supply chains requires significant resources and expertise.

- **Language and Cultural Barriers:** Operating in foreign countries can present challenges in terms of communication and understanding local customs.
- **Safety Risks:** Investigators may face risks such as hazardous working conditions or political instability.

Conclusion

Undercover operations are a specialized tool that can be highly effective in addressing complex corporate challenges. However, they must be conducted with careful planning, ethical considerations, and legal compliance. By combining undercover investigations with other investigative techniques, organizations can strengthen their security posture and protect their assets.

CHAPTER SEVENTEEN

The Undercover Operation and Entrapment

One of the most complex legal and ethical challenges in the realm of undercover operations is the concept of entrapment. Entrapment occurs when law enforcement or private investigators induce a person to commit a crime that they would not otherwise have committed. This is a critical issue because it undermines the integrity of the legal system and can lead to wrongful convictions.

The Line Between Investigation and Inducement

Distinguishing between legitimate investigative techniques and entrapment can be difficult. The key lies in determining whether the individual had the predisposition to commit the crime or was coerced or persuaded by the investigator.

- **Predisposition:** If an individual was already inclined to commit a crime, and the sevestigator merely provided an opportunity, it generally does not constitute entrapment.

- **Inducement:** If the investigator creates a criminal opportunity or persistently persuades an otherwise unwilling person to commit a crime, it may be considered entrapment.

Case Studies

- **United States v. Russell (1973):** The Supreme Court established a subjective test for entrapment, focusing on the defendant's predisposition to commit the crime.
- **Soriano v. United States (1984):** The Court clarified that government conduct must be "shocking to the conscience" to constitute entrapment.

Mitigating the Risk of Entrapment
To avoid entrapment, investigators must:

- **Avoid creating criminal opportunities:** Focus on identifying and investigating existing criminal activities rather than creating new ones.
- **Document thoroughly:** Maintain detailed records of all interactions with potential suspects to demonstrate predisposition.
- **Adhere to ethical guidelines:** Develop clear guidelines for undercover operations to prevent overzealous tactics.
- **Seek legal counsel:** Consult with legal experts to ensure compliance with all applicable laws.

By understanding the complexities of entrapment and adhering to strict ethical standards, organizations can conduct undercover operations effectively while protecting their legal and reputational interests.

Types of Surveillance in Manufacturing

Surveillance in the manufacturing industry is a crucial component of ensuring security, quality, and efficiency. It involves the systematic observation of processes, people, and assets to identify potential risks, improve operations, and protect the business.

Asset Protection

- **Perimeter Surveillance:** Protecting the facility's boundaries from unauthorized entry. This includes using CCTV cameras, access control systems, and alarms to monitor entry and exit points.
- **Internal Surveillance:** Monitoring warehouse and storage areas to prevent theft, damage, or loss of raw materials, finished goods, and machinery. The use of CCTV cameras, motion detectors, and RFID tags can help track assets.
- **Inventory Management:** Utilizing surveillance to track inventory levels, identify discrepancies, and prevent stockouts or overstocks.

Example: A large automotive manufacturing plant in Pune uses CCTV cameras and motion detectors to monitor its warehouse, protecting high-value components and finished vehicles from theft.

Quality Control

- **Production Line Monitoring:** Using surveillance to observe production processes, identify defects, and ensure adherence to quality standards.
- **Product Inspection:** Implementing visual inspection systems to detect product defects and inconsistencies.

- **Traceability:** Tracking products through the production process to identify the source of any quality issues.

Example: A food processing plant in Punjab uses CCTV cameras to monitor the production line, ensuring hygiene standards are maintained and products meet quality specifications.

Safety and Security

- **Workplace Safety:** Monitoring for potential hazards, such as spills, equipment malfunctions, or unsafe working conditions.
- **Access Control:** Controlling entry and exit points to prevent unauthorized access and protect employees.
- **Emergency Response:** Using surveillance to monitor for emergencies, such as fires or accidents, and to coordinate response efforts.

Example: A chemical manufacturing plant in Gujarat employs CCTV cameras and fire detection systems to monitor the facility for safety hazards and to ensure a quick response in case of emergencies.

Production Optimization

- **Performance Monitoring:** Tracking equipment performance, identifying bottlenecks, and optimizing production schedules.
- **Workforce Optimization:** Analyzing employee movements and activities to improve efficiency and productivity.
- **Energy Management:** Monitoring energy consumption to identify opportunities for savings.

Example: A textile mill in Tamil Nadu uses surveillance data to analyze production line efficiency, identifying bottlenecks and optimizing resource allocation.

Challenges and Considerations

- **Privacy Concerns:** Balancing the need for surveillance with employee privacy rights.
- **Data Management:** Managing and storing large volumes of surveillance data.
- **False Alarms:** Minimizing false alarms to avoid unnecessary disruptions.
- **Cost:** Investing in surveillance systems and maintaining them can be expensive.
- **Ethical Considerations:** Ensuring that surveillance is used ethically and responsibly.

By effectively implementing surveillance systems and addressing these challenges, manufacturing companies can significantly improve security, quality, and efficiency.

CHAPTER EIGHTEEN

Surveillance: A Double-Edged Sword

Surveillance, the close observation of a person, place, or thing, is a tool with immense potential benefits but also significant ethical and legal implications. In the corporate world, it's employed for a variety of purposes, including employee monitoring, competitive intelligence, and asset protection.

Employee Activity Surveillance

The monitoring of employee behavior has become increasingly common due to concerns about productivity, security, and fraud.

- **Purpose:**

  - Detect theft, fraud, or embezzlement
  - Identify security breaches or data leaks
  - Monitor employee productivity and performance
  - Prevent workplace violence or harassment

- **Methods:**

- Computer monitoring: Tracking keystrokes, websites visited, and emails.
  - Video surveillance: Observing employee activities in common areas and workspaces.
  - Time and attendance tracking: Monitoring employee hours and breaks.

- **Ethical Considerations:**

  - Privacy concerns: Balancing the need for surveillance with employee privacy rights.
  - Employee morale: Excessive surveillance can lead to decreased morale and job satisfaction.
  - Legal compliance: Adhering to labor laws and data protection regulations.

Example: A tech company might monitor employee internet usage to prevent data leaks and protect intellectual property. However, indiscriminate monitoring could lead to privacy concerns and stifle employee creativity.

Competitor Analysis Through Surveillance

Gaining insights into competitors' operations can provide a competitive edge. Surveillance plays a crucial role in this process.

- **Purpose:**

  - Identify new products or services
  - Analyze marketing strategies
  - Assess pricing and promotional activities
  - Understand competitor strengths and weaknesses

- **Methods:**

- Physical surveillance of competitor facilities
- Online monitoring of competitor websites and social media
- Analysis of competitor marketing materials and advertising
- Reverse engineering of competitor products

- **Ethical Considerations:**

  - Industrial espionage: Avoiding activities that cross the line into illegal or unethical territory.
  - Trade secrets: Respecting competitor intellectual property.
  - Public image: Maintaining a positive corporate reputation.

Example: A retail company might use surveillance to observe a competitor's store layout, customer traffic patterns, and merchandising displays to inform its own store planning.

Asset Protection Through Surveillance

Protecting physical assets from theft, vandalism, and other threats is essential for businesses. Surveillance systems play a vital role in deterring and detecting criminal activities.

- **Purpose:**

  - Prevent theft and vandalism
  - Monitor access control
  - Detect fire or other hazards
  - Provide evidence for insurance claims

- **Methods:**

  - CCTV cameras: Monitoring premises and capturing footage of incidents.
  - Access control systems: Limiting entry to authorized personnel.
  - Alarm systems: Detecting intruders and unauthorized access.

- **Ethical Considerations:**

  - Privacy concerns: Balancing security needs with the privacy rights of employees and customers.
  - False alarms: Minimizing the frequency of false alarms to avoid unnecessary disruptions.

Example: A manufacturing plant might use surveillance cameras to monitor the production floor, warehouse, and perimeter to deter theft and protect equipment.

Legal and Ethical Implications

Surveillance, while a valuable tool, raises significant legal and ethical concerns. Companies must carefully balance the need for security and efficiency with the rights of employees, customers, and competitors.

- **Privacy laws:** Adhering to data protection regulations is essential.
- **Employee consent:** Obtaining explicit consent for monitoring employee activities is often required.
- **Ethical guidelines:** Developing clear policies and procedures for surveillance activities.
- **Public image:** Avoiding practices that could damage the company's reputation.

By carefully considering these factors and implementing appropriate safeguards, organizations can leverage surveillance effectively while minimizing risks.

CHAPTER NINETEEN

Challenges in Implementing Surveillance Programs

While surveillance offers significant benefits, its implementation is fraught with challenges. Here's a deeper dive into some of the key issues:

Technological Challenges

- **Data Overload:** The sheer volume of data generated by surveillance systems can be overwhelming. Efficient data management and analysis tools are essential.
- **False Positives and Negatives:** Surveillance systems can generate a high number of false alarms, leading to wasted resources and potential legal issues.
- **Privacy Concerns:** Balancing the need for surveillance with individual privacy rights requires careful consideration of data collection and storage methods.
- **Cost:** Implementing and maintaining surveillance systems can be expensive, particularly for small businesses.

Legal and Ethical Challenges

- **Legal Compliance:** Organizations must adhere to data protection laws, labor regulations, and other legal frameworks.
- **Employee Morale:** Excessive surveillance can lead to decreased employee morale, trust, and productivity.
- **Public Image:** Improper use of surveillance can damage a company's reputation.
- **Ethical Considerations:** Surveillance raises ethical questions about the balance between security and privacy.

Operational Challenges

- **System Integration:** Integrating surveillance systems with other security and business systems can be complex.
- **Personnel Training:** Employees need proper training to effectively use and interpret surveillance data.
- **Incident Response:** Developing effective procedures for responding to incidents detected through surveillance is crucial.
- **Continuous Improvement:** Surveillance systems require regular evaluation and updates to remain effective.

Mitigating Challenges
To address these challenges, organizations can:

- **Focus on Data Privacy:** Implement robust data protection measures and comply with relevant regulations.

- **Transparent Communication:** Clearly communicate surveillance policies to employees.
- **Ethical Guidelines:** Develop and adhere to ethical guidelines for surveillance use.
- **Regular Reviews:** Conduct periodic assessments of surveillance programs to ensure effectiveness and compliance.
- **Employee Training:** Provide training on surveillance policies and procedures.
- **Technology Investment:** Invest in advanced surveillance technologies that can improve accuracy and reduce false alarms.
- **Data Retention Policies:** Establish clear guidelines for data retention and disposal.

By carefully considering these challenges and implementing appropriate measures, organizations can effectively leverage surveillance to enhance security while protecting privacy and maintaining a positive work environment.

CHAPTER TWENTY

Surveillance in the IT Industry

The IT industry, characterized by intellectual property, sensitive data, and rapid technological advancements, heavily relies on surveillance to protect its assets and maintain a competitive edge.

Types of Surveillance in the IT Industry

- **Employee Monitoring:**

  - Keystroke logging: Recording keystrokes to detect potential data breaches or intellectual property theft.
  - Email and internet monitoring: Tracking employee online activities to prevent misuse of company resources and identify potential threats.
  - Time and attendance tracking: Monitoring employee work hours and productivity.

- **Insider Threat Detection:**

  - Identifying potential threats from within the organization through behavioral analysis and anomaly detection.

- Monitoring access to sensitive data and systems.

- **Cybersecurity Surveillance:**

  - Detecting and responding to cyberattacks, such as malware, phishing, and DDoS attacks.
  - Monitoring network traffic for suspicious activities.

- **Intellectual Property Protection:**

  - Tracking the usage and distribution of intellectual property to prevent unauthorized access or misuse.

Technology in IT Surveillance

The IT industry is at the forefront of surveillance technology development and implementation.

- **Intrusion Detection and Prevention Systems (IDPS):** These systems monitor network traffic for suspicious activity and can block attacks.
- **Security Information and Event Management (SIEM):** This technology collects, analyzes, and correlates log data from various sources to identify security threats.
- **User and Entity Behavior Analytics (UEBA):** This analyzes user and system behavior to detect anomalies that may indicate malicious activity.
- **Data Loss Prevention (DLP):** This technology prevents sensitive data from being copied, printed, or sent outside the organization.

Challenges and Considerations

- **Privacy Concerns:** Balancing the need for security with employee privacy is a critical challenge.
- **Legal Compliance:** Adhering to data protection laws and regulations is essential.
- **False Positives:** Surveillance systems can generate a high number of false alarms, requiring careful analysis.
- **Employee Morale:** Excessive monitoring can negatively impact employee morale and productivity.
- **Ethical Considerations:** The ethical implications of surveillance must be carefully considered.

Best Practices

- **Transparency:** Clearly communicate surveillance policies to employees.
- **Purpose Limitation:** Collect and use data only for legitimate purposes.
- **Data Minimization:** Collect only the necessary data.
- **Data Retention:** Implement data retention policies to limit the storage of sensitive information.
- **Employee Training:** Educate employees about security threats and their role in protecting company assets.
- **Regular Review:** Continuously evaluate surveillance practices to ensure effectiveness and compliance.

By carefully considering these factors and implementing appropriate measures, IT organizations can effectively use surveillance to protect their assets and mitigate risks while respecting employee privacy and legal requirements.

CHAPTER TWENTY-ONE

Surveillance in the Manufacturing Industry

The manufacturing industry is a prime candidate for surveillance due to the high value of assets, the potential for theft and vandalism, and the need for efficient operations.

Types of Surveillance in Manufacturing

- **Asset Protection:**

  - Protecting raw materials, finished goods, and machinery from theft, damage, or loss.
  - Monitoring warehouse and storage areas for unauthorized access.

- **Quality Control:**

  - Ensuring product quality and compliance with standards.
  - Identifying production process inefficiencies.

- **Safety and Security:**

- ○ Monitoring for workplace hazards and accidents.
- ○ Detecting security breaches and unauthorized personnel.

- **Production Optimization:**

  - ○ Tracking equipment performance and identifying maintenance needs.
  - ○ Optimizing production processes and workflow.

25. Surveillance Technologies in Manufacturing

- **CCTV:** Traditional but still effective for monitoring entry points, production areas, and storage facilities.
- **Access Control Systems:** Restricting access to authorized personnel and tracking movements within the facility.
- **IoT Sensors:** Monitoring environmental conditions, equipment performance, and product quality.
- **Drones:** For large-scale outdoor surveillance of facilities and surrounding areas.
- **Video Analytics:** Using AI to analyze video footage for anomalies and incidents.

Challenges and Considerations

- **Privacy Concerns:** Balancing surveillance needs with employee privacy rights.
- **Data Management:** Managing large volumes of surveillance data efficiently.
- **False Alarms:** Minimizing false alarms to avoid unnecessary disruptions.

- **Cost:** Investing in surveillance systems and maintaining them can be expensive.
- **Employee Morale:** Excessive surveillance can negatively impact employee morale.

Best Practices

- **Clear Surveillance Policy:** Establish guidelines for surveillance use and employee awareness.
- **Data Privacy:** Protect employee privacy and comply with data protection regulations.
- **Risk Assessment:** Identify areas of highest risk to prioritize surveillance efforts.
- **Training:** Train employees on surveillance procedures and their role in security.
- **Regular Review:** Evaluate the effectiveness of surveillance systems and make necessary adjustments.

Case Studies

- **Automotive Manufacturing:** Surveillance is used to protect expensive machinery, prevent theft of intellectual property, and monitor production lines for efficiency.
- **Food Processing:** Surveillance helps ensure food safety, prevent contamination, and protect against theft.
- **Electronics Manufacturing:** Protecting sensitive components and preventing industrial espionage are key concerns.

By implementing effective surveillance systems and addressing potential challenges, manufacturing companies can enhance security, improve efficiency, and protect their assets.

CHAPTER TWENTY-TWO

Surveillance Technologies in Manufacturing

Surveillance technology has become an indispensable tool for modern manufacturing operations, enhancing security, efficiency, and quality control. Let's delve deeper into specific technologies and their applications.

CCTV (Closed-Circuit Television)

- **Core Functionality:** Real-time video monitoring of a defined area.
- **Applications in Manufacturing:**

  - Perimeter security: Preventing unauthorized access.
  - Production floor monitoring: Observing production processes, identifying bottlenecks, and ensuring worker safety.
  - Warehouse surveillance: Detecting theft, damage, or unauthorized access.
  - Quality control: Monitoring product assembly and packaging.

Example: A pharmaceutical company uses CCTV to monitor sterile production areas, ensuring adherence to stringent hygiene standards.

Access Control Systems

- **Core Functionality:** Restricting access to authorized personnel and tracking movements within a facility.
- **Applications in Manufacturing:**

  - Controlling entry and exit points.
  - Monitoring access to sensitive areas, such as research labs or control rooms.
  - Tracking employee attendance and productivity.

Example: A semiconductor manufacturing plant implements a card-based access control system to restrict entry to cleanrooms and protect intellectual property.

IoT Sensors

- **Core Functionality:** Collecting data from physical devices and environments.
- **Applications in Manufacturing:**

  - Monitoring equipment health: Detecting anomalies in machine performance to prevent breakdowns.
  - Tracking inventory levels: Ensuring optimal stock levels and preventing shortages.
  - Environmental monitoring: Measuring temperature, humidity, and air quality in production areas.

Example: A food processing plant uses IoT sensors to monitor temperature and humidity levels in storage areas, ensuring product quality and safety.

Drones

- **Core Functionality:** Aerial surveillance and data collection.
- **Applications in Manufacturing:**

  - Facility inspections: Identifying potential safety hazards or structural issues.
  - Inventory management: Conducting aerial surveys of stockpiles.
  - Security patrols: Monitoring perimeter security and detecting unauthorized activity.

Example: A large-scale manufacturing plant uses drones to inspect the exterior of buildings for damage, such as roof leaks or structural weaknesses.

Video Analytics

- **Core Functionality:** Analyzing video content to extract information and insights.
- **Applications in Manufacturing:**

  - Object detection and tracking: Identifying people, vehicles, or objects in video footage.
  - Behavior analysis: Detecting unusual or suspicious activities.
  - Facial recognition: Identifying authorized personnel.

Example: A manufacturing plant uses video analytics to detect unauthorized personnel entering restricted areas or to identify equipment malfunctions based on abnormal visual patterns.

By effectively combining these technologies, manufacturing companies can significantly enhance security, efficiency, and quality control. However, it's essential to balance the benefits of surveillance with privacy concerns and ethical considerations.

CHAPTER TWENTY-THREE

Video Analytics: The Intelligence Behind the Camera

Video analytics has emerged as a critical component of modern surveillance systems, transforming raw video footage into actionable intelligence. By applying advanced algorithms and artificial intelligence, video analytics can extract valuable insights from video data, enhancing security, efficiency, and decision-making.

Core functionalities of video analytics

- **Object Detection and Tracking:** Identifying and following objects within a video frame, such as people, vehicles, or products.
- **Behavior Analysis:** Recognizing patterns of behavior, such as loitering, theft, or aggression.
- **Facial Recognition:** Identifying individuals based on facial features.
- **License Plate Recognition (LPR):** Identifying and tracking vehicles based on their license plates.

- **Anomaly Detection:** Identifying unusual or suspicious activities.

Applications in Manufacturing

- **Quality Control:** Detecting defects in products, monitoring production line efficiency, and ensuring worker safety.
- **Security:** Identifying unauthorized access, detecting theft, and monitoring for suspicious activities.
- **Inventory Management:** Tracking the movement of goods within a warehouse.
- **Predictive Maintenance:** Predicting equipment failures based on video analysis of machine behavior.

Challenges and Considerations

- **Data Privacy:** Ensuring compliance with data protection regulations and minimizing privacy intrusions.
- **False Positives and Negatives:** Balancing the accuracy of the system with the risk of false alarms.
- **Computational Resources:** Video analytics can be computationally intensive, requiring powerful hardware and software.
- **Ethical Implications:** Considering the potential misuse of facial recognition and other advanced analytics.

Future Trends

- **AI Integration:** Deeper integration of artificial intelligence for more sophisticated analysis and decision-making.

- **Real-time Analytics:** Processing video data in real-time to enable immediate response to incidents.
- **Edge Computing:** Performing video analytics at the edge of the network for faster processing and reduced bandwidth consumption.
- **Privacy-Preserving Analytics:** Developing techniques to protect privacy while extracting valuable insights from video data.

By leveraging video analytics, manufacturing companies can significantly enhance their security, efficiency, and overall operations. However, it is essential to implement these technologies responsibly and ethically, considering the potential impacts on individuals and society.

CHAPTER TWENTY-FOUR

Challenges in Implementing Surveillance Systems

While surveillance technology offers significant benefits, implementing and managing these systems effectively presents various challenges.

Technical Challenges

- **Data Management:** The vast amount of data generated by surveillance systems requires efficient storage, management, and analysis.
- **Video Quality:** Ensuring optimal video quality for accurate analysis and evidence preservation can be challenging.
- **System Integration:** Integrating surveillance systems with other IT infrastructure, such as access control and alarm systems, can be complex.
- **False Alarms:** Minimizing false alarms is crucial to avoid resource wastage and maintain system effectiveness.

Operational Challenges

- **Staff Training:** Ensuring that personnel are adequately trained to operate and maintain surveillance systems.
- **Privacy Concerns:** Balancing security needs with employee and customer privacy rights.
- **Cost Management:** Optimizing the surveillance system to achieve maximum return on investment.
- **System Maintenance:** Regular system updates and maintenance to ensure optimal performance.

Best Practices for Implementation

- **Needs Assessment:** Clearly define the objectives of the surveillance system.
- **Technology Selection:** Choose the appropriate surveillance technologies based on specific needs.
- **Data Retention Policy:** Establish guidelines for data storage and deletion.
- **Privacy Impact Assessment:** Conduct a thorough assessment to identify potential privacy risks.
- **Employee Training:** Provide comprehensive training to personnel involved in surveillance operations.
- **Regular Review:** Conduct periodic audits to evaluate the system's effectiveness.
- **Incident Response Plan:** Develop procedures for responding to incidents captured on surveillance footage.

By addressing these challenges and following best practices, organizations can maximize the benefits of surveillance systems while minimizing risks.

Ethical Implications of Facial Recognition in Manufacturing

Facial recognition technology, a subset of video analytics, has seen rapid advancement and widespread adoption across industries, including manufacturing. While offering potential benefits in terms of security and efficiency, it also raises significant ethical concerns.

Privacy Concerns

- **Consent:** The collection and use of facial biometric data without explicit and informed consent raises serious privacy concerns.
- **Data Retention:** Storing facial recognition data for extended periods poses risks of misuse and unauthorized access.
- **Surveillance Overreach:** The potential for excessive surveillance and tracking of individuals without legitimate justification.

Discrimination and Bias

- **Algorithmic Bias:** Facial recognition systems can exhibit biases based on race, gender, and other demographic factors, leading to inaccurate or discriminatory outcomes.
- **False Positives and Negatives:** Errors in facial recognition can lead to wrongful accusations or missed identifications.

Security Risks

- **Data Breaches:** The theft of facial recognition data can lead to identity theft and other forms of fraud.
- **Deepfakes:** Malicious actors can create deepfake videos to manipulate public perception and damage

reputations.

Legal and Regulatory Challenges

- **Data Protection Laws:** Compliance with data protection regulations, such as GDPR and CCPA, is essential.
- **Liability:** Determining liability in case of false positives or negative impacts on individuals.
- **Government Oversight:** The need for clear regulations and oversight to prevent misuse of facial recognition technology.

To mitigate these challenges, organizations implementing facial recognition technology should:

- **Prioritize Privacy:** Obtain explicit consent, minimize data collection, and implement robust data protection measures.
- **Conduct Regular Audits:** Assess the system for biases and inaccuracies.
- **Transparency:** Be transparent about facial recognition use and data handling practices.
- **Employee Training:** Educate employees about the technology and its limitations.
- **Ethical Guidelines:** Develop clear ethical guidelines for facial recognition use.

By carefully considering these ethical implications and implementing appropriate safeguards, organizations can harness the benefits of facial recognition technology while minimizing risks.

CHAPTER TWENTY-FIVE

Overcoming the Challenge of False Positives in Surveillance Systems

False positives, or instances where a surveillance system incorrectly identifies a threat or anomaly, are a significant challenge in the effective operation of surveillance systems. These errors can lead to wasted resources, damage to reputation, and erosion of trust.

Understanding False Positives

False positives occur due to several factors:

- **System Sensitivity:** Overly sensitive systems may detect minor fluctuations as threats.
- **Environmental Factors:** External factors like weather, lighting, or physical obstructions can trigger false alarms.
- **Data Quality:** Poor image or video quality can lead to inaccurate analysis.

- **Algorithm Limitations:** Imperfections in the algorithms used for detection can contribute to false positives.

Mitigating False Positives

- **Fine-tuning Algorithms:** Continuously improving the accuracy of detection algorithms through machine learning and data analysis.
- **Adjusting Sensitivity:** Balancing the need for high detection rates with the risk of false alarms.
- **Data Quality Improvement:** Ensuring high-quality video and image data through proper system maintenance and calibration.
- **Verification Processes:** Implementing human verification to confirm alerts before taking action.
- **False Positive Analysis:** Tracking and analyzing false positives to identify patterns and improve system performance.
- **Contextual Awareness:** Incorporating contextual information, such as time of day, weather conditions, and historical data, to reduce false alarms.

Balancing Security and Privacy

While reducing false positives is crucial, it's essential to maintain a balance with security requirements. Overly aggressive filtering to reduce false positives might lead to missed threats. Therefore, a careful approach is necessary.

By implementing these strategies, organizations can significantly reduce false positives while maintaining the effectiveness of their surveillance systems.

CHAPTER TWENTY-SIX

False Positives in the Financial Industry

The financial industry is particularly sensitive to false positives in surveillance systems. Given the high-stakes nature of financial transactions, any errors in detection can lead to significant reputational damage, financial losses, and legal repercussions.

Challenges Unique to Finance

- **Regulatory Compliance:** Financial institutions operate in a highly regulated environment, and false positives can lead to regulatory scrutiny and penalties.
- **Customer Impact:** Incorrectly flagging customers as potential fraudsters can damage customer relationships and lead to lost business.
- **Operational Efficiency:** Excessive false positives can overwhelm investigation teams, impacting operational efficiency.
- **Reputation Risk:** Publicly known instances of false positives can damage a financial institution's reputation.

Examples of False Positives in Finance

- **Fraud Detection Systems:** Flagging legitimate transactions as fraudulent, leading to declined payments and customer inconvenience.
- **Insider Threat Detection:** Incorrectly identifying employees as potential threats, leading to morale issues and productivity losses.
- **Market Surveillance:** Falsely identifying market manipulation or insider trading, impacting investor confidence.

Mitigating False Positives in Finance

- **Continuous Monitoring and Refinement:** Regularly evaluating the performance of surveillance systems and making adjustments as needed.
- **Human-in-the-Loop Verification:** Incorporating human oversight to review alerts and reduce false positives.
- **Customer Education:** Communicating with customers about fraud prevention and the potential for false positives.
- **Balancing Security and Customer Experience:** Finding the right balance between security measures and customer convenience.
- **Regulatory Compliance:** Ensuring that surveillance systems comply with all relevant regulations.

By carefully managing false positives, financial institutions can protect their customers, maintain operational efficiency, and preserve their reputation.

CHAPTER TWENTY-SEVEN

False Positives in the Insurance Industry

False positives in the insurance industry occur when legitimate claims or policyholders are mistakenly flagged as fraudulent. This can lead to significant consequences for both the insurer and the policyholder.

Types of False Positives in Insurance

- **Claim Fraud Detection:** Legitimate claims being incorrectly flagged as fraudulent, leading to delayed or denied payments.
- **Policyholder Screening:** Incorrectly identifying low-risk policyholders as high-risk, resulting in increased premiums or denied coverage.
- **Anti-Money Laundering (AML) Screening:** Flagging legitimate transactions as suspicious, leading to unnecessary investigations and customer inconvenience.

Impact of False Positives

- **Customer Dissatisfaction:** False positives can damage customer relationships, leading to churn and negative word-of-mouth.

- **Increased Costs:** Investigating and resolving false positives can be time-consuming and expensive.
- **Regulatory Risks:** High false positive rates can attract regulatory scrutiny.
- **Operational Efficiency:** False positives can disrupt claims processing and other operational activities.

Mitigating False Positives

- **Data Quality:** Ensuring accurate and complete data is essential for reducing false positives.
- **Algorithm Refinement:** Continuously improving fraud detection models to enhance accuracy.
- **Human Review:** Implementing a human-in-the-loop process to verify alerts.
- **Customer Communication:** Clearly communicating the reasons for investigations and providing timely updates.
- **False Positive Analysis:** Tracking and analyzing false positives to identify patterns and improve system performance.

By effectively managing false positives, insurance companies can improve customer satisfaction, reduce costs, and protect their reputation.

CHAPTER TWENTY-EIGHT

False Positives in Cybersecurity

The cybersecurity industry is particularly susceptible to false positives due to the complex nature of threats and the need for rapid detection.

Types of False Positives in Cybersecurity

- **Intrusion Detection Systems (IDS):** Flagging legitimate network traffic as malicious.
- **Anti-Virus Software:** Incorrectly identifying harmless files as viruses.
- **Fraud Prevention Systems:** Misclassifying legitimate transactions as fraudulent.

Impact of False Positives in Cybersecurity

- **Increased Alert Fatigue:** A high volume of false positives can overwhelm security teams, leading to decreased responsiveness to actual threats.
- **Operational Disruptions:** False positives can disrupt business operations, such as blocking legitimate email or network traffic.

- **Loss of Trust:** Frequent false positives can erode trust in security systems and lead to complacency.
- **Financial Loss:** Investigating and responding to false positives can be time-consuming and costly.

Mitigating False Positives in Cybersecurity

- **Continuous Monitoring and Tuning:** Regularly adjusting system parameters to optimize performance.
- **Whitelisting:** Creating a list of trusted applications and files to reduce false positives.
- **User Education:** Training employees to recognize phishing attempts and other social engineering tactics.
- **Incident Response Planning:** Having clear procedures for investigating and responding to alerts.

By implementing these strategies, organizations can significantly reduce the impact of false positives on their cybersecurity operations.

Section 4: Screening and Due Diligence

1. Application of Screening in Business Practice
2. Screening as a Corporate Safeguard
3. In-House Screening vs. Professional Investigators
4. Screening in the Entertainment Industry
5. Customer Due Diligence (CDD) in the Financial Services Industry
6. Screening in Litigation Support Services
7. The Advantages of Employing a Private Investigator for Corporate Investigations

Application of Screening in Business Practice

Screening is a critical process in various business functions, from hiring to product development. It involves evaluating and selecting the most suitable options from a pool of alternatives.

Screening in Human Resources

- **Applicant Screening:** Evaluating resumes, cover letters, and application forms to identify qualified candidates for job openings.
- **Background Checks:** Verifying candidate information, such as employment history, education, and criminal records.
- **Drug Testing:** Screening potential employees for substance abuse.
- **Reference Checks:** Contacting previous employers to assess a candidate's work performance.

Screening in Product Development

- **Idea Screening:** Evaluating new product concepts to prioritize those with the highest potential for success.
- **Concept Testing:** Gathering feedback on product concepts to identify areas for improvement.
- **Prototype Screening:** Assessing product prototypes to ensure they meet design specifications and customer needs.

Screening in Marketing

- **Market Research:** Identifying target markets and customer segments.
- **Advertising Screening:** Evaluating the effectiveness of advertising campaigns.
- **Customer Feedback:** Analyzing customer reviews and feedback to identify areas for improvement.

Screening in Finance

- **Investment Screening:** Evaluating potential investment opportunities based on financial performance, risk, and alignment with investment goals.
- **Credit Risk Assessment:** Assessing the creditworthiness of individuals or businesses.
- **Fraud Prevention:** Screening transactions for suspicious activity.

Screening in Supply Chain Management

- **Supplier Screening:** Evaluating potential suppliers based on factors such as quality, cost, and ethical practices.

- **Product Quality Screening:** Inspecting incoming materials and products for defects.
- **Risk Assessment:** Identifying potential risks in the supply chain, such as supply disruptions or counterfeit products.

Benefits of Effective Screening

- **Improved Decision Making:** By focusing on the most promising options, screening helps businesses make better decisions.
- **Reduced Risk:** Identifying and mitigating potential risks early in the process.
- **Increased Efficiency:** Streamlining processes and saving time and resources.
- **Enhanced Customer Satisfaction:** Providing products and services that meet customer needs and expectations.

Effective screening requires a combination of human judgment and data analysis. By implementing robust screening processes, businesses can increase their chances of success and mitigate potential risks.

CHAPTER THIRTY

Screening as a Corporate Safeguard

Screening, in its various forms, serves as a critical bulwark against potential risks and threats to a corporation. It is a proactive measure to ensure the integrity of the organization, its operations, and its reputation.

Safeguarding Human Capital

- **Talent Acquisition:** Rigorous screening prevents the hiring of unsuitable candidates who could pose a security risk, be involved in fraudulent activities, or simply be a poor cultural fit.
- **Employee Retention:** Regular screening, especially in roles handling sensitive data, helps identify potential issues before they escalate into major problems.

Protecting Corporate Reputation

- **Supplier Screening:** Ensuring that suppliers adhere to ethical and legal standards prevents association with businesses involved in harmful practices.
- **Customer Screening:** In certain industries (like finance or insurance), screening customers helps prevent fraud

and money laundering.

Safeguarding Financial Health

- **Financial Screening:** Identifying potential financial risks associated with customers, suppliers, or partners.
- **Fraud Prevention:** Detecting anomalies in financial transactions to prevent losses.

Mitigating Legal Risks

- **Compliance Screening:** Ensuring adherence to industry regulations and laws.
- **Risk Assessment:** Identifying potential legal issues and taking preventive measures.

Enhancing Operational Efficiency

- **Quality Control Screening:** Identifying defective products or services before they reach the market.
- **Supply Chain Screening:** Ensuring the integrity of the supply chain and preventing disruptions.

Specific Examples:

- A technology company conducts rigorous background checks on employees handling sensitive data to prevent intellectual property theft.
- A pharmaceutical company screens suppliers for adherence to quality and safety standards to protect consumers.
- A financial institution employs sophisticated fraud detection systems to identify suspicious transactions.

In conclusion, screening is a multifaceted tool that contributes significantly to corporate safeguarding. By identifying potential risks and vulnerabilities early on, organizations can protect their reputation, financial stability, and overall success.

CHAPTER THIRTY-ONE

In-House Screening vs. Professional Investigators

The decision to conduct screening in-house or outsource it to a professional investigator is a critical one for businesses. Each approach has its advantages and disadvantages.

In-House Screening

- **Advantages:**

  - Cost-effective for small-scale operations.
  - Greater control over the screening process.
  - Potential for faster turnaround times.
  - Alignment with company culture and values.

- **Disadvantages:**

  - Limited resources and expertise.
  - Potential for bias or favoritism.
  - Time-consuming for HR staff.
  - Risk of overlooking critical information.

Example: A small tech startup might conduct initial applicant screening in-house to quickly filter resumes based on specific technical skills.

Professional Investigator

- **Advantages:**

  - Expertise in investigative techniques and data analysis.
  - Access to specialized databases and resources.
  - Objectivity and impartiality.
  - Compliance with legal and regulatory requirements.

- **Disadvantages:**

  - Higher costs.
  - Reliance on external resources.
  - Potential for slower turnaround times.

Example: A large financial institution might outsource background checks to a professional investigator to ensure thoroughness and compliance with anti-money laundering regulations.

Factors to Consider

- **Company size and resources:** Smaller companies may opt for in-house screening due to cost constraints, while larger organizations might benefit from outsourcing.
- **Industry regulations:** Certain industries, such as finance and healthcare, have strict screening requirements that might necessitate professional assistance.

- **Complexity of screening:** Extensive background checks or specialized investigations often require the expertise of a professional investigator.
- **Time constraints:** If rapid turnaround times are critical, outsourcing might be preferable.

Hybrid Approach

Many organizations combine in-house screening with external investigations. This hybrid approach allows for cost-effective initial screening while leveraging the expertise of professionals for more complex cases.

Ultimately, the decision to conduct screening in-house or outsource depends on the specific needs of the organization and the resources available.

CHAPTER THIRTY-TWO

Screening in the Entertainment Industry

The entertainment industry, characterized by high competition, intellectual property, and public image concerns, relies heavily on effective screening processes.

Types of Screening in Entertainment

- **Talent Screening:** Identifying and selecting actors, musicians, models, and other performers based on their skills, appearance, and marketability.
- **Content Screening:** Evaluating scripts, music, and other creative content for suitability, legality, and potential impact.
- **Background Checks:** Verifying the backgrounds of talent, employees, and partners to mitigate risks.
- **Financial Screening:** Assessing the financial viability of projects and partners.

Challenges and Best Practices

- **Subjectivity:** Assessing talent or creative content often involves subjective judgments.

- **Competition:** The highly competitive nature of the industry requires efficient and effective screening processes.
- **Legal and Ethical Considerations:** Adhering to labor laws, copyright regulations, and ethical standards.
- **Changing Trends:** Staying updated with evolving audience preferences and industry standards.

Best practices include:

- **Clear Criteria:** Defining specific criteria for talent or content selection.
- **Multiple Evaluators:** Involving diverse perspectives in the screening process.
- **Data Analysis:** Using analytics to identify trends and patterns in successful projects.
- **Continuous Improvement:** Regularly reviewing and refining screening processes.

Case Study: Child Actor Safety

The entertainment industry has faced scrutiny regarding the treatment of child actors. Rigorous screening of child performers, including background checks on parents or guardians, is essential to protect their well-being.

CHAPTER THIRTY-THREE

Customer Due Diligence (CDD) in the Financial Services Industry

Customer Due Diligence (CDD) is a critical component of anti-money laundering (AML) and counter-terrorist financing (CTF) compliance. It involves the verification of customer identity and the understanding of their business activities.

Core Components of CDD

- **Customer Identification:** Gathering accurate and verifiable information about the customer, including name, address, date of birth, and government-issued identification.
- **Customer Verification:** Confirming the information provided by the customer through independent sources.
- **Beneficial Ownership:** Identifying the individuals who ultimately own or control a legal entity.

- **Risk Assessment:** Evaluating the customer's risk profile based on factors such as occupation, geographic location, and transaction patterns.
- **Ongoing Monitoring:** Continuously monitoring customer relationships and transactions for suspicious activity.

Challenges in CDD

- **Customer Complexity:** Dealing with complex corporate structures and beneficial ownership can be challenging.
- **Regulatory Changes:** Keeping up with evolving AML/CTF regulations can be burdensome.
- **Customer Experience:** Balancing the need for thorough CDD with the customer experience.
- **Technological Advancements:** Leveraging technology effectively while managing data privacy concerns.

Best Practices for CDD

- **Risk-Based Approach:** Focusing CDD efforts on high-risk customers.
- **Technology Utilization:** Employing advanced tools for customer identification and verification.
- **Employee Training:** Ensuring staff is well-versed in CDD procedures and regulations.
- **Continuous Improvement:** Regularly reviewing and updating CDD processes.
- **Collaboration:** Sharing information with other financial institutions and law enforcement agencies.

Case Study: Correspondent Banking

Correspondent banking involves financial institutions maintaining accounts with each other to facilitate cross-border transactions. Effective CDD is crucial to prevent these accounts from being misused for money laundering or terrorist financing. Challenges include identifying beneficial owners of correspondent banks, assessing their risk profiles, and monitoring transaction activity.

By implementing robust CDD procedures, financial institutions can significantly reduce the risk of financial crime while maintaining customer relationships.

CHAPTER THIRTY-FOUR

Screening in Litigation Support Services

Litigation support services rely heavily on screening to gather, analyze, and present evidence effectively. The process involves meticulously examining vast amounts of data to identify relevant information, potential inconsistencies, and patterns.

Types of Screening in Litigation Support

- **Document Review:** Analyzing legal documents, emails, and other electronic data to extract relevant information.
- **Witness Identification and Interview:** Screening potential witnesses to assess their knowledge and credibility.
- **Expert Witness Selection:** Evaluating the qualifications and expertise of potential expert witnesses.
- **Data Analysis:** Screening large datasets to identify trends, patterns, and anomalies.
- **Electronic Discovery:** Screening electronically stored information (ESI) to identify relevant data for production.

Challenges and Best Practices

- **Overwhelming Volume:** Litigation often involves massive amounts of data, requiring efficient screening methods.
- **Relevance Assessment:** Determining which information is truly relevant to the case can be challenging.
- **Privilege Review:** Identifying privileged information and protecting attorney-client privilege.
- **Technology Utilization:** Employing advanced technology, such as artificial intelligence and machine learning, to enhance screening efficiency.

Best practices include:

- **Early Case Assessment:** Conducting a thorough initial assessment to define the scope of the case.
- **Technology Adoption:** Using e-discovery platforms and advanced analytics tools.
- **Team Collaboration:** Fostering collaboration between legal and support teams.
- **Quality Control:** Implementing rigorous quality control measures to ensure accuracy.
- **Continuous Improvement:** Regularly evaluating and refining screening processes.

Case Study: Complex Commercial Litigation

In a high-stakes commercial litigation case involving multiple parties and vast amounts of data, effective screening is crucial. By using advanced e-discovery tools and a team of experienced reviewers, legal teams can identify key documents, analyze witness testimony, and build a strong case.

Screening in litigation support is an essential component of successful case management. By employing efficient and accurate screening processes, legal teams can improve case outcomes and reduce costs.

"investigative" or "forensic" methods. These methods involve diligent and systematic examination of evidence to uncover facts and support legal arguments.

Investigative Techniques in Litigation Support

Here are some of the investigative techniques employed in litigation support:

- **Forensic Accounting:** Analyzing financial records to detect fraud, embezzlement, or other financial irregularities.
- **Digital Forensics:** Recovering deleted data, reconstructing events, and preserving electronic evidence.
- **Investigative Interviewing:** Conducting interviews with witnesses and parties involved in the case.
- **Document Analysis:** Thoroughly reviewing documents to identify inconsistencies, contradictions, or hidden information.
- **Database Searches:** Utilizing public and private databases to gather information relevant to the case.

Example: Investigating Financial Fraud

In a case of alleged financial fraud, investigative techniques might involve:

- Forensic accounting to trace the flow of funds and identify discrepancies.

- Digital forensics to recover deleted emails or financial records.
- Interviewing employees, customers, and third parties to gather information.
- Analyzing financial statements and other documents for anomalies.
- Using database searches to identify potential accomplices or related fraudulent activities.

While these techniques are essential for uncovering evidence, they are conducted openly and transparently, subject to legal and ethical guidelines.

CHAPTER THIRTY-FIVE

The Advantages of Employing a Private Investigator for Corporate Investigations

The integration of investigative techniques into corporate operations, as outlined previously, underscores the need for specialized expertise and resources. Employing a private investigator offers several distinct advantages.

Specialized Expertise

- **Deep Investigative Skills:** Private investigators possess a unique skill set honed through years of experience in gathering, analyzing, and presenting evidence.
- **Industry Knowledge:** Many investigators specialize in specific industries, providing in-depth understanding of industry-specific challenges and risks.

- **Network of Contacts:** Established relationships within relevant industries can expedite investigations.

Objectivity and Independence

- **Unbiased Perspective:** Private investigators can provide an unbiased view of a situation, free from internal pressures or conflicts of interest.
- **Confidentiality:** Maintaining client confidentiality is a core principle of the profession.
- **Independence:** Private investigators can operate independently, without being influenced by corporate politics or hierarchies.

Resource Efficiency

- **Specialized Tools and Technology:** Private investigators have access to advanced investigative tools and software.
- **Time Savings:** Experienced investigators can quickly identify key areas of investigation and prioritize efforts.
- **Cost-Effective Solutions:** By focusing on critical issues, private investigators can help companies avoid unnecessary expenses.

Risk Mitigation

- **Legal and Ethical Compliance:** Private investigators are familiar with the legal and ethical boundaries of investigations.
- **Crisis Management:** They can be deployed rapidly to respond to crises and protect the company's reputation.

- **Reputation Protection:** By uncovering potential threats or misconduct, private investigators can help safeguard the company's image.

Case Examples

- **Intellectual Property Theft:** A private investigator can conduct undercover operations, surveillance, and digital forensics to identify and protect a company's intellectual property.
- **Employee Fraud:** An experienced investigator can uncover embezzlement, theft, or other forms of employee misconduct.
- **Due Diligence:** Private investigators can conduct comprehensive background checks on potential business partners or acquisition targets.

While in-house investigations have their place, employing a private investigator offers a specialized and objective perspective that can be invaluable in complex and sensitive cases.

Legal and Regulatory Framework

1. Changes Brought by the Bhartiya Sakshya Sanhita

1. Changes Brought by the Bhartiya Sakshya Sanhita (21)

This structure provides a logical progression from foundational concepts to specific applications and challenges. It also groups related topics together for easier understanding and analysis.

Changes Brought by the Bhartiya Sakshya Sanhita

Changes Brought by the Bhartiya Sakshya Sanhita

The Bharatiya Sakshya Sanhita (BSS), or the Indian Evidence Act, 2023, is a significant overhaul of the previously existing Indian Evidence Act, 1872. The primary aim of this new legislation is to align the Indian legal system with the advancements in technology and societal changes.

Key Changes Introduced by the BSS

1. **Inclusion of Electronic Evidence:**

   - One of the most significant changes is the explicit recognition of electronic evidence as primary evidence.
   - The definition of 'document' has been expanded to include electronic records, ensuring that digital evidence is given equal weight as physical documents.

- This is a crucial step in addressing the challenges posed by the digital age and ensuring that courts can effectively deal with electronic evidence.

2. **Oral Evidence:**

- The BSS allows for oral evidence to be given electronically, which is a departure from the traditional mode of in-person testimony.
- This change is in line with the increasing use of technology in legal proceedings and can enhance accessibility and efficiency.

3. **Expert Evidence:**

- The BSS has introduced provisions for the appointment of expert witnesses by the court, which can enhance the accuracy and reliability of expert testimony.
- This is a step towards improving the quality of expert evidence and ensuring that it is based on sound scientific principles.

4. **Confidentiality and Privilege:**

- The BSS has clarified the concept of privilege, particularly in relation to communications between lawyers and clients.
- It also addresses the issue of confidentiality in the context of electronic communications.

5. **Other Changes:**

- ◦ The BSS has made several other changes, including modifications to provisions on relevancy of facts, admissions, and burden of proof.
- ◦ The aim of these changes is to improve the clarity and effectiveness of the evidence law.

Impact of the BSS

The BSS is expected to have a profound impact on the Indian legal system by:

- **Facilitating the use of technology:** The inclusion of electronic evidence and the provision for electronic testimony will make the legal process more efficient and accessible.
- **Enhancing the quality of evidence:** By providing clear guidelines for the admissibility and evaluation of evidence, the BSS aims to improve the accuracy and reliability of legal decisions.
- **Protecting rights:** The provisions on confidentiality and privilege are designed to safeguard the rights of individuals and organizations.

While the BSS is a significant step forward, its implementation will require time and adaptation by the legal community. It is expected that the full impact of the new law will be evident in the coming years.

The Bharatiya Sakshya Sanhita (BSS), or the Indian Evidence Act, 2023, is a significant overhaul of the previously existing Indian Evidence Act, 1872. The primary aim of this new legislation is to align the Indian legal system with the advancements in technology and societal changes.

Glossary: -

General Management Terms

- **Contingency Management:** A managerial approach that emphasizes adaptability and flexibility in response to changing circumstances.
- **Due Diligence:** A comprehensive investigation or audit of a potential investment or business transaction.
- **Lateral Thinking:** A problem-solving method that involves exploring multiple possible solutions.
- **Screening:** The process of evaluating and selecting candidates, products, or services based on specific criteria.
- **Surveillance:** The close observation of a person, place, or thing.

Investigative Terms

- **Covert Operation:** A clandestine activity conducted to gather intelligence or information.
- **Undercover Operation:** A specific type of covert operation where an individual assumes a false identity.
- **Surveillance:** The systematic observation of people, places, or things.
- **Due Diligence:** A thorough investigation of a person, business, or situation.
- **Forensic Accounting:** The application of accounting and investigative techniques to detect and prevent fraud.
- **Digital Forensics:** The recovery and investigation of material found in digital devices.

Legal and Ethical Terms

- **Intellectual Property:** Intangible assets such as patents, trademarks, and copyrights.
- **Privacy:** The right of individuals to control their personal information.
- **Data Protection:** Measures to protect personal information from unauthorized access, use, disclosure, destruction, or modification.
- **Ethical Hacking:** The practice of penetrating a computer system on behalf of the owner to find security vulnerabilities.

Other Terms

- **Risk Management:** The process of identifying, assessing, and controlling potential risks to an organization.
- **Corporate Governance:** The system of rules, practices, and processes by which a company is directed and controlled.
- **Human Resources:** The department responsible for managing an organization's workforce.
- **Supply Chain:** The network of individuals, organizations, activities, information, and resources involved in moving a product or service from supplier to customer.

Relevant Resources For The Book

Primary Sources

- **Case Studies:** Real-world examples of successful and failed investigations, corporate strategies, and crisis management.
- **Legal Precedents:** Court rulings and legal frameworks related to corporate investigations, privacy, and data protection.
- **Industry Reports:** Market research and industry analyses to provide context and trends.
- **Government Data:** Statistical data on crime, fraud, and economic indicators.

Secondary Sources

- **Academic Research Papers:** Studies on management, leadership, psychology, and criminology.
- **Books and Articles:** Publications on corporate investigations, security, and risk management.
- **Industry Publications:** Trade journals and magazines focused on specific industries.
- **News and Media Reports:** Current events and case studies to illustrate concepts.

Additional Resources

- **Government Websites:** Websites of regulatory bodies and law enforcement agencies.
- **Industry Associations:** Websites of industry-specific associations and chambers of commerce.

- **Think Tanks and Research Institutes:** Publications and reports from organizations focused on management, security, and ethics.
- **Online Databases:** Academic databases, legal databases, and news archives.

Specific Resource Examples

- **Case Studies:** Enron, Satyam, and the 2008 financial crisis.
- **Legal Precedents:** Indian Evidence Act, Information Technology Act, and relevant case laws.
- **Industry Reports:** Reports from Gartner, Forrester, and McKinsey on industry trends.
- **Government Data:** Crime statistics from the National Crime Records Bureau (NCRB).
- **Academic Research:** Studies on leadership, organizational behavior, and criminology from Harvard Business Review, McKinsey Quarterly, and academic journals.

By leveraging a combination of these resources, the book can provide a comprehensive and insightful exploration of the topics covered.

* 9 7 9 8 8 9 5 1 9 7 1 6 5 *